Don't Get a Job ...
Make a Job

Don't Get a Job ... Make a Job

How to make it as a creative graduate

Gem Barton

Published in 2016 by
Laurence King Publishing Ltd
361–373 City Road
London EC1V 1LR
United Kingdom
T +44 20 7841 6900
F +44 20 7841 6910
enquiries@laurenceking.com
www.laurenceking.com

Reprinted 2016

A catalogue record for this book is available
from the British Library.

ISBN: 978-1-78067-746-0

Book design: Turnbull Grey
Project editor: Gaynor Sermon
Infographics: Russell Bell

Printed in China

"A new generation of young business owners are leading the way out of the downturn, according to the annual Simply Business Start-up Index, which reveals a 29% increase in firms started by 18–25 year olds since the recession took hold in 2008."
(*Simply Business*, UK, May 2013)

"… with 58% raising less than £1,000 to get off the ground and 39% managing on less than £500."
(*Simply Business*, UK, May 2013)

Don't Get a Job, <u>Make a Job</u>

Introduction

First things first—the days of trading in your degree certificate for a nice safe job offer are gone, and who knows if they will ever return? It is simply not enough to graduate anymore; the world demands more from you—you are the future, you are the next generation of entrepreneurs, design-thinkers, hyper-specialists, and cultural agitators. You have a role, you have a responsibility. It is no longer just about the world of the design … it is about the design of your world!

You will be aware that the prospect of "finding work" is tough. You have heard nothing but horror stories since the economic downturn began in 2008, yet you still chose a design degree, you are still chasing that dream. Why? Because secretly, deep down, you know that the future will be led by free-thinking, forward-looking, rule-bending, problem-solving, question-asking social-radicals, that's why! Think about the biggest problems we face today: poverty, dwindling energy resources, and war—it is design, not money, that has the potential to solve these problems.

Our educated youth are ethical souls; they want to make a living, sure, but they also want to leave a legacy of betterment behind them for future generations, not just a collection of pretty things to be listed and honoured and drooled over in class. They are a powerful force, one that doesn't plan on waiting for clients to commission them—they will be busy setting mousetraps of design excellence, subverting the balance of power away from those with the cash and toward those with the design ability. They are a hungry, motley, self-initiated crew, taking the world of work into their own hands. Gone are the days of "getting a job" and welcomed is the age of "making a life".

Since 2008 and the global economic collapse, when the banks virtually stopped lending, the majority of businesses and individuals as a result became more risk averse. This had quite an apocalyptic effect on the approach to securing work in the design industry. In such times of difficulty, as often happens, diamonds form from the charcoal—this so very trying situation has spawned a generation of fierce go-getters. And now that the floodgates have been opened, the design job market will never be the same again! No one can say for sure that it was the recession alone that inspired this shift, but if it had not been the recession it would have been something else, eventually. The natural instinct for change and reactionary progress will always be present in the creative industries.

There is a long history in the design world of trailblazers—the rare few who, for fear or fashion, feel the need to radicalize the process, but prior to 2008 the conventional route into practice was DEGREE>CV>FOLIO>INTERVIEW>JOB. A sensible equation that, if followed, would almost certainly get you a job, somewhere. There were always the few who had secured work experience in summer breaks, impressed people, kept in touch, and been offered some work straight after graduation—but most of us simply followed the rules and hoped to goodness that in the end we would be fruitful. Many were indeed lucky, until the jobs dried up, and it was then that the strong and the inventive found new ways to approach clients, to set up practice, to specialize, diversify, and subvert the traditions. While a terrifying time to be in the midst of, this is the time when new traditions are made, legends begin, and the clock restarts.

By way of strategy-driven chapters, this book tells the stories of the new-generation trailblazers within our changing world; we explore their strategies, get introduced to their working methods, and hear exactly how and why they chose to make their own way. You will hear the stories behind the inception of designers and founders from all around the world, including behind-the-scenes looks at Something & Son, The Draftery, The Glue Society, Vin & Omi, Le Creative Sweatshop, and Stereotank. You will also hear from those who have been there, done that, and donated the T-shirt, relating first-hand experiences and offering expert advice—read on to get this exclusive guidance from Jimenez Lai, Studio Weave, Jason Bruges, and others.

The book is NOT a how-to guide. You are advised against simply copying ideas from the bright sparks featured here. The book has been written with the intention of educating and inspiring you, to open your eyes to the myriad opportunities available. If there is only one piece of information you take away from reading this book, let it be this: if you cannot find an opportunity that you like/want, then you owe it to yourself to make your own!

As a former student of architecture in the UK, now with almost a decade of experience in teaching different design courses around the country, I have a unique insight into the world of both design practice and education. Having entered the architecture profession after graduating in 2006, I myself followed the "traditional" DEGREE>CV>FOLIO>INTERVIEW>JOB route, securing a job in a medium-size practice. Less than 18 months later, and just three months before my final accreditation exams, I received my first redundancy letter. As a relatively new graduate, I was a victim of the last-one-in, first-one-out trap. Like many of the case studies featured in the book, I knew that tough decisions had to be made; I saw this negative as an opportunity to "irritate the oyster", to make my own way and find—no, create—the perfect job for me. This took years and generated many tears along the way. I experienced a crisis of confidence brought about by the fear of the unknown, so I stuck to what I knew, I rinsed my (then-small) network of contacts and quite simply persevered. I took jobs I despised, doing work I did not enjoy in order to make ends meet, and I dedicated all my free time to making work, meeting new people, and developing my personal brand.

Jeff Bezos, founder of Amazon, famously said, "Your personal brand is what people say about you when you are not in the room". I tried my hand at everything I could and then curated my working life based on my experiences. Today I spread my time between teaching, writing, designing, building, show-making, and living. This recipe for working will not suit everyone, nor will it appear in the index of a careers manual, but for many like me, being in control of their destiny, being flexible, with the ability to spread risk, respond quickly, and do something different every day is of the utmost importance.

I had goals, one of which was to write a book, to help others through some of the tough times I had experienced, and to reassure all those who don't fit the little job-shaped boxes that it is all going to be OK. In fact it's going to be great. Boxes are for the ordinary, and who wants to be ordinary? The sooner I learned that not wanting the same things as everyone else made me unique, the sooner I realized I could become anything I wanted, even an author. What at one time I had perceived as my weakness ultimately became my best strength.

In researching the content and case studies for this book I have scoured the globe for individuals taking their lives into their own hands. I have conducted interviews with every person in this book (and many more), as well as quizzing academics and leading industry professionals. I have rinsed my (now considerably larger) network of contacts and drained every single favour. This book is the culmination of 18 months of hard work, late nights, thousands of e-mails, and a lot of fun. This book adds to a much broader debate around the world about the future of design education. It takes a first-hand approach to collecting evidence from those on the front line, the hard data as well as emotions, gut reactions, and instincts—those respected commodities of design practice—and questions how this data can be applied to the education system, learning from the realities of a recession-hit world and proposing amendments to education practice to ensure graduates are better prepared for such eventualities in the future. Never before has a piece of research crossed the globe in such a personal way, offering up selfless examples to inspire the new generation in the design world—to inspire you!

Don't Get a Job, <u>Make a Job</u>

Propaganda

Design firms receive an abundance of CVs and applications daily. So what can be done to make yours stand out? Most people put "creative and hard-working" on their CV, but there is no better way to get that message across than to *show* an employer how creative and hard-working you really can be. Young people around the globe are becoming more and more imaginative in making themselves seen and heard, ensuring that potential employers and clients really understand just how creative they are.

Your personal brand is powerful; it is what makes you who you are and, in a tough market, the first hurdle is making sure that you are seen and remembered. So how do you make yourself visible in such a competitive industry?

The following case studies use ingenious techniques akin to propaganda, a form of communication aimed at influencing the attitudes of people toward a specific cause or position ... in this case, selling themselves to others.

Strategy:
Put Yourself Out There

Skyler Fike

A proactive young man, Skyler Fike used the graphics skills he learned in architecture school and applied them to the production of a pamphlet as a unique tactic to "sell himself". His bold approach to networking and face-to-face meeting sets him apart from the inundation of faceless e-mails and printed folios that design studios receive daily. While this line of attack may not be appropriate for all employers and prospective employees, taking the time to research and identify his ideal work placement, coupled with his confidence to put himself out there, can clearly be seen to have been an effective method for Skyler.

Being mindful of your own goals and limitations is very important. Working for free for an unspecified length of time is not encouraged. Prearranging a time period and task list during which your suitability for the firm can be assessed could be an option. Skyler knew that during the economic recession he might have to do some work for free, but he set appropriate limitations based on his own financial status as well as his principles. Putting agreements in place before shaking hands on a deal ensures that everyone involved knows where they stand and prevents any confusion once the contract period is over. Don't be afraid of stating your intentions for a work placement, such as indicating any specific skills you would like to learn. This shows that you are a focused and dedicated young designer.

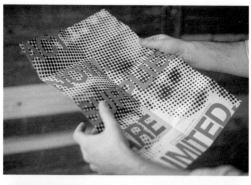

"Don't be afraid of stating your intentions for a work placement."

Gem Barton

Free Intern pamphlet

Experience

My approach to the working world has been less traditional than my college classmates and other colleagues. After college I started by working for free at a local firm, which seemed to be the only viable option, given that unemployment was so high at the time. I had essentially given up on finding work when a mentor of mine encouraged me to research architecture firms in the city, walk directly into the offices of those firms that I liked, ask to speak to the partner, and tell them I would work for free. While ethically I don't really agree with the idea of free work, it opened many doors that would have never otherwise opened, or at least opened so quickly.

As my method of execution, I researched firms and their partners and used fold-up pamphlets to display as much information as possible about my work, without being overwhelming or arduous. For each of the respective partners whose firms I walked into, I personalized every aspect of the process; casual firm, casual dress. At busy architects practices, I would stop by after 6pm, when things were shutting down (or just getting started!). I researched pictures of partners (if their website had them) and kept an eye out for architects I might possibly recognize at an event.

What happened next

I progressed into working for even more architects, but this time as a paid freelance worker. As I had hoped, the freelance position turned into a full-time job for a year and a half with another firm. By that time, two years later, I had either met, worked for, or become closely acquainted with many of the major architects in the city.

Free can't sustain itself for more than a short time, so I only worked for free for about eight weeks. The Free Intern pamphlet turned into the Cheap Intern pamphlet and I began round two of walking into firms looking for part-time freelance work. Basically the same thing happened; I got 10 to 20 hours a week of work for each of the four or five architects that hired me. I worked freelance at offices and at home for about four months until I was hired full-time by an architect to whom I'd given a pamphlet four months prior but never heard back from.

Now I work freelance for various architects in Dallas, Texas, while shooting photography on the side and taking on other personal design projects as time permits.

"Free can't sustain itself for more than a short time, so I only worked for free for about eight weeks. The Free Intern pamphlet turned into the Cheap Intern pamphlet."

Skyler Fike

Mam's Fridge Gallery

Strategy:

Release early, release often

Matthew Britton

In a packed creative world, Matthew Britton manages to innovate every day. He uses social media and his unique online projects to share his ideas and thoughts, and to connect with artists, gallerists, and more. He is his own unique selling point. The creative market is a competitive one—finding young designers open to sharing thoughts and ideas (for free) is not commonplace, and this is what makes Matthew stand out as being different.

Much of Matthew's work is light-hearted and tongue-in-cheek; it makes people smile, which is more than half the battle. There is a great deal to be said for engaging potential clients and employers early on in the development of your work. Allowing others to see how your ideas grow enables them to become invested in you and understand your process—people like what is familiar to them. But be careful not to give away too much. You own your ideas when they are in your head, be smart about how much you share.

Out of Office, 2014

"I realized that by being brave and putting out content that actively critiques the system by which we operate, you can gain more exposure than any council-funded scheme."

Matthew Britton

Experience

The majority of my time was spent applying for pre-existing opportunities and I felt that this time would be better spent in devising new methods of gaining employment, whether this would be through self-funding projects or simply being innovative about how I could bring exposure to my practice.

I think that you can become too reliant upon what the art world offers you and forget that you are as much an active component of it as its funding bodies. I still don't quite understand why you would have to so thoroughly outline what you would like funding for, before you are granted the funds to do it—it seems to contradict the creative process entirely.

What happened next

I became really interested in alternative modes of production. This led to the development of microcuratorial projects such as Mam's Fridge Gallery and Out of Office, where I have been fortunate enough to work with a variety of like-minded and active practitioners from around the world. I consider collaboration to be an important method of seeking employment; it has helped me to gain further collaborative work as well as contacts at other arts initiatives. These projects have led on to further opportunities in roles as a facilitator in workshops for several arts organizations. I believe that it is due to the exposure from self-directed projects that I was able to employ roles that better suited my skill-set; the positions required me to respond to given circumstances from the role of a new media artist. I think I would have been waiting a long time to see that printed as a job vacancy, but it was because of the previous projects that I was contacted directly to conduct freelance work.

Advice

I would suggest that you be as prolific as possible and make sure your work is as accessible as you are willing. In terms of my own drive, I ensure that my output is pretty constant and that the audience is as much a part of its development as my own thought process. I swear by and deploy the software philosophy of "release early, release often" with regard to being creative. I believe that work is critiqued and sculpted by its viewer and that you shouldn't be afraid of these interactions.

It is important that the working relationship is mutually beneficial and that your interactions are clearly understood.

Be active in the current dialogue of your chosen medium. Some would refer to this as having your finger on the pulse but I would describe it as not allowing the stream to swallow you up.

I believe I have grown because of my somewhat naive interpretation of the art world. It is important to ask questions of the system and not just go along with its rules.

"He doesn't rely on a CV to prove how creative he is—he shows people!"

Gem Barton

Skip YouTube

Don't be daunted by self promotion

Advice on propaganda from Alec Dudson,
Founder and Editor, *Intern* magazine

Self-promotion is something that I long considered an undesirable necessity. For years, the idea of talking myself up in order to convince someone I was the bee's knees was one that I felt principled against. I wanted no part in these slippery and egotistical undertakings and figured that if people liked me and wanted to work with me, they would; if they didn't, they wouldn't.

Then I chanced upon an industry that I wanted to work in and my simplistic and clichéd concepts had to evolve. Having studied sociology to master's level and decided that my tryst with academia had run its course, I was working full-time in the bars that I worked part-time in during university. My amateurish exploration of photography as a means of creative output had stemmed from one of the units on my MA, and a post-graduation trip around the US left me with my first major body of work. I'd received some encouraging feedback about the photos and when invited to start a website with some friends, effectively made my first step toward self-promotion in the creative sphere. That (now-defunct) website went on to become a means of building my profile.

Initially, I mainly posted my own photographic output, but as the months passed I became interested in posting the work of others and interviewing them via e-mail about it. My time away from the bar increasingly became consumed by the site and having seen a couple of the other guys secure internships in the magazine industry using the website we had started as a reference, I built up the courage to give it a go. From having absolutely no background or agency in the creative sphere, in the space of eight months I had convinced the online editor at Domus that my self-taught "editorial experience and knowledge of WordPress" rendered me a worthy pair of extra hands on campus.

What I came to realize at that point was that I had proven my initial theory about self promotion wrong. I hadn't done any sucking up, stabbed anyone in the back, or lied—I'd simply done something for myself and as such was in control of the rules. The ability and confidence to be self-sufficient goes a long way to helping you stand out from the pack. The wider importance of that skill-set is evidenced by the fact that 43 percent of creative workers in the UK are self-employed compared to just 13 percent of the overall economy, according to a recent survey by Creative Blueprint.

The cynics among you, and, trust me, on this point I was one of you, will simply call this a "blag", but there is a difference and that is "substance". By being confident in what you have done and talking to others about it, you will find that they feel more inclined to collaborate with you, employ you, and recommend you to others. I maintain that it is tremendously important to conduct yourself morally and try not to step on others to get ahead. Doing a job well is only one part of working in the creative industries; there are more people than ever out there who also have the skills to do the job. Your personality is your biggest weapon and no matter what way you dress it up (or down), as a creative, your personality becomes your brand.

When I started *Intern* magazine and got to the stage where finance was required, I turned to Kickstarter, a crowdfunding platform for creative projects. Extensive research proved that as "creator", I would have to inspire confidence in potential backers through as many means as possible. Effectively, when backing any crowdfunding project, an investor may be intrigued by the idea, but the creator is the person that delivers it and, as such, it's them that the investor is taking a gamble on. From there on, I responded to every press enquiry I could, spoke at every event I could, and made sure that all of these interactions were broadcast via social media. My personal "brand" was growing. Self promotion has allowed me to find new work and collaborate on really inspiring projects.

Don't be daunted by the concept of self promotion. You can be loud and proud about your work without being egotistical; if you don't tell people you're there, they aren't going to find you.

Don't Get a Job, <u>Make a Job</u>

Going mobile

Many young professionals are seeing the benefits in turning the tables on the conventional approach to winning work, such as entering competitions and bidding for commissions. If these methods aren't for you, then what are the alternatives?

The following case studies introduce some creatives who have used innovative methods of showcasing their skills and talents outside of the usual environments by taking themselves and their ideas to the streets. Doing this increases your visibility and puts your work in front of people who may never otherwise have come across you and discovered how fantastic you are. Going public in this way has endless benefits, but it is not easy!

Subverting the idea of the traditional approach is energetic and proactive but it can also be difficult to sustain—can this gimmick work as a lone venture or does it need to be a part of a greater master plan?

Strategy:

Go to the clients, don't make them come to you

icecream architecture

Having identified their goals early, the members of icecream architecture shrewdly took a separate academic course in business alongside their architecture studies. If you are thinking of setting up alone, then getting extra knowledge outside of your own discipline can be extremely valuable. Being able to balance your books as well as please clients and appease planners is extremely important.

If your business is consultation, then being able to visit and speak with the community is a top priority. icecream's van is essentially a mobile and highly approachable office—it is not so much about being big and beautiful (although that surely helps), but rather, more about accessibility and visibility. Choosing a fun, community-friendly icon such as an ice cream van—a vehicle we all have fond childhood memories of—was an astute decision. Having a hook that is a perfect match for your business needs as well as a strong brand identity is the ideal situation to put yourself in. Verging on performativity at times, the van, the activity, the display and exchange of knowledge and ideas attracts attention, inquisition, and footfall—the kind of attention large corporations pay marketing firms big bucks to achieve. On the following pages Sarah Frood explains how the company got itself on the road.

Fort William

Experience

icecream architecture was established in 2009—after completing an intensive business-training course alongside our master's in architecture we stepped out and bought our van. The primary aim was not necessarily about getting noticed, but the van was a metaphor suggesting that, just like the ice cream van that enters communities providing a service on a daily basis, we would also take our services out to the community. At this point our drive was to approach architecture in a different way and, in doing so, also approach how we secured work and where we secured work. The exposed nature of the van instantly removed any barrier that might prevent people from approaching us. Though our experience was limited at this point we had a view on how most things should function both socially and economically. Our initial clients were looking for a more engaged method of practice, a way to better understand what the communities that they were working in needed or wanted.

"The exposed nature of the van instantly removed any barrier that might prevent people from approaching us."

Sarah Frood

What happened next

The van quickly became a hook and a tool for engagement. It took us out of town halls and into the streets, and in a very practical way our ethos as a practice was personified by our brand and by the van. Its positioning during the work we undertook made the projects that we were working on more visible but also advertised icecream architecture to a new market, allowing a word-of-mouth growth to build on our initial contracts, and allowing our experience and the scale of work that we undertook to reach the required levels to enter the competitive tender market.

"Having a hook that is a perfect match for your business needs as well as a strong brand identity is the ideal situation to put yourself in."

Gem Barton

Opposite top: Govan Book of Memories, Glasgow
Bottom: Public AA Strategy and Town Centre Chavette Denny, Falkirk
Below: Beyond the Fishing Line, Social Enterprise start-up incubator, Glasgow

Strategy:

Go guerrilla

Alma-nac Collaborative Architecture

Considering your future career as an integral part of your life is tantamount to success. Starting your own practice can be hard, stressful work, but it is greatly rewarding if done well. Being aware of this in advance and being fully prepared for what lies ahead can help you avoid problems in the long term.

Alma-nac did just this. They carefully considered their options, knowing that leaving good jobs in the midst of the recession, with no clients to speak of, would be tough. In order to put themselves in front of as many people as possible (potential future clients) they went guerrilla—setting up a stall offering "Free Architecture" on one of London's most trafficked streets. As this was a clandestine operation, they took a risk and did not seek the necessary permissions, which was dangerous, as getting caught out before they had even begun was not a part of the plan! The public was charmed by Alma-nac's conversation, knowledge, and determination, and in turn Alma-nac learned a lot about the people, their understanding of architecture, and their passion for cities. Win, win. They even converted some of the compliments they received into paying jobs. All from a folding table and a few posters.

Big things are possible when you believe in what you are doing, and the public respond well to seeing young people working tirelessly to follow and fulfil their dreams. Perhaps not everyone will be as lucky as Alma-nac, but by learning from their process, as described here by Chris Bryant, you too can take the public by storm.

Free Architecture

Experience

We started the practice in 2009, mid-recession, leaving good jobs but with limited experience and without clients. We carried with us a lot of energy, optimism, and a good amount of naivety—which can be quite useful in the early stages as it tends to force learning through doing rather than doubting or overly questioning ideas before they begin to grow. We had decided to start our own practice because we desired autonomy and wanted to design a practice as a key component of our lives that reflected our values and allowed us to pursue projects that interested us. A key part of this was to be building early on rather than confined to only "paper architecture".

The lack of clients was obviously a significant problem when starting. We didn't want to focus on competitions because they resemble a lottery, with very limited client contact, no guarantee of the winning design being built, and they often don't generate very much (if any) income. It's worth pointing out that we were in a position where we had to earn money to pay the rent and keep us fed.

Our answer was "Free Architecture"—a guerrilla stall (guerrilla in the sense that we didn't seek permission) offering free design consultation to anyone that wanted it. The stall was set up on several Saturdays at various busy locations in London, including Portobello Road and the Southbank. The idea was to get out of the office and engage with the people that we would be working with and make it easy for them to talk to an architect. The results far exceeded our expectations. Many people were just intrigued by what we were doing and would more often than not congratulate us on the idea. A good proportion wanted to discuss architecture, often passionately and with a good deal of knowledge. Some thought it was a free architecture tour and a select few thought we were offering free buildings! All of this (including the more eccentric and lengthy conversations) only helped to strengthen our feeling that the general public cared very much about design and the city, and that by setting up our own practice we had made the right decision. After each day we felt tired but energized by the discussions and elated by the compliments. On top of this we were getting five to ten consultation requests per day. We knew that these wouldn't all turn into projects but it gave us the opportunity to gain experience at pitching and understand what clients were looking for.

What happened next

As it turned out, some of our first built projects came from initial discussions at our stall. These projects have led to further commissions and we now have a portfolio of work that continues to win us jobs.

"Free Architecture" put us in contact with hundreds of people, taught us about clients, gave us many thought-provoking conversations, and won us the projects that started the firm. All of that from a budget of £70 to set up a stall with some posters.

Advice

Our experience is that we learn most when we act on our ideas rather than question them to death. The act of doing is more satisfying, enjoyable, and worthy than the act of thinking about doing. Don't become overly jealous of what others are involved with, and try instead to forge your own path.

"We wanted to get out there and meet people. Not everyone knows what an architect does or how to approach them. We broke down that barrier by going into the street and inviting people for informal conversations."

Chris Bryant

Don't Get a Job, <u>Make a Job</u>

Strategy:

Bend the rules

Hank Buttita

For many, the need and desire to debunk the corporate, hierarchical job structure begins while still in education—feeling the grip of the institution can be an inspiration to challenge formalization, manipulate design briefs, and stretch expectation. Enter Hank Buttita.

Preferring to make rather than draw, Hank charmed his tutor into allowing him to build his final design project rather than simply represent it through models and drawings. He invested US$3,000 of his own money—at any age this is a huge risk—showing the sheer passion and determination he had for his work. The completed project was picked up on inspiration websites across the globe. Hank believes that by bending the rules and being different he became noticeable, and being noticeable is a very useful commodity. Whether your desire is to get a job or to impress a client, the extended network that being a familiar name grants you is priceless.

Hank was entrepreneurial, keeping at the forefront his own designs for his future career, and with that he hit the road, en route catching the attention of the global press.

"Without stepping outside the norm to build my thesis rather than draw it, not only would I have gone unnoticed, I would have been unnoticeable."

Hank Buttita

Experience

In architecture school I was tired of drawing buildings that would never exist, for clients that were imaginary, with details I didn't fully understand. I prefer to work with my hands, exploring details thoroughly, and enjoy working/prototyping at full scale. So for my master's final project, rather than design a space that would never exist, I took a financial and academic risk by purchasing a used school bus for $3000, and over the course of the semester I converted it into a tiny living space. I developed a presentation that focused not on the bus itself, but discussed the value of design through building and questioned the largely conceptual nature of architectural education.

Converting the space in less than four months was physically and mentally exhausting and nearly financially ruinous, but the risk and hard work paid off handsomely. The press generated by the project ultimately established my reputation and launched my career, connecting me with my first architectural clients.

After graduation, I teamed up with a friend who is a professional photographer to take the bus on a maiden voyage across the western United States. Through his fantastic photography we were able to spread the story of the bus and its conversion to people around the globe, expanding awareness of the tiny house movement and demonstrating the potential for small spaces to be both beautiful and functional.

What happened next

Over the course of seven years of architectural education, I came to realize that architecture is not the profession I imagined it to be. In order to stay engaged, I needed a certain level of hands-on interaction in design that doesn't currently exist. I wanted to prototype, and I wanted to build.

After graduation, instead of applying to firms I leased warehouse space and set up a small wood shop, centred around an old, beat-up 4x8 CNC machine. I have since been piecing together a freelance design career, tackling a variety of design and fabrication work to establish my business and stay afloat.

I was "that guy" who spends all his time in the shop. Students looked to me for help with their models, structures, and mechanics, professors hired me as a research assistant to develop solar ducts, and now I'm teaching a materials course at my alma mater, and my peers come to me for their digital fabrication needs.

Without stepping outside the norm to build my thesis rather than draw it, not only would I have gone unnoticed, I would have been unnoticeable. It's true that one of the most important parts of college is networking, especially in design. The goal of networking is to become a familiar name and get your foot in the door; even in the twenty-first century it is the most reliable way to find an employer or a client.

Now, with a unique, recognizable project to my name, my network has grown exponentially, connecting me with other professionals and potential clients all over the planet.

Hank Bought a Bus

You don't have to reinvent the wheel

<u>Advice on going mobile from David Chambers</u>
<u>& Kevin Haley, aberrant architecture</u>

Buildings are notoriously stationary things. Rooted to the ground with heavy materials, the architecture we live, work, and play in is somewhat opposed to our increasingly mobile, fluid, cloud-based daily experience.

As mobile buildings occupy no single place permanently, the absence of any planning considerations means that perhaps greater, more risky, designs are ventured. Material and colour palettes can also be more adventurous, colourful, and attention grabbing than their more permanent relations, essential for any young practice trying to make a name for itself and maximize its exposure. Mobile commissions can also be delivered relatively quickly, enabling a portfolio of built work to be speedily assembled.

Our first mobile project was the Tiny Travelling Theatre, which gave its debut performance at the 2012 Clerkenwell Design Week in London. The mobile theatre toured the Clerkenwell area for the duration of the festival, towed to various staging sites from Clerkenwell Green in north London to St. John's Square in the south.

Once in position, an audience of up to six people could sit inside the theatre's enclosed stage and seating area and enjoy a series of intimate one-off theatrical, comedy, and musical performances delivered by solo performers, but often with audience participation. A large sound funnel provided passersby with a glimpse of the acts within. Meanwhile, folding tables and ice buckets on the exterior allowed visitors to enjoy pre- and post-performance drinks at the impromptu bar.

The itinerant nature of mobile projects means that the spatial experience of your work can potentially be exposed to a far wider audience than perhaps would be possible if your project was tied to one place. For example, the Tiny Travelling Theatre has subsequently popped up at many other locations around the UK including last year at the Queen Elizabeth Olympic Park at an event that enabled thousands of new people to experience the project.

While the Tiny Travelling Theatre was conceived as a "pop-up" temporary project, another one of our mobile projects, the Roaming Market, which we created for Lower Marsh Market in Waterloo, was imagined as a more permanent piece of architecture that happened to be movable. The Roaming Market can be moved to different sites around Waterloo much like the Tiny Travelling Theatre moved around Clerkenwell. Once in situ, the compact structure unfolds into a multifunctional market stall, featuring a covered seating area with built-in chessboard and a stage on the roof for hosting live events and performances.

You do not literally have to reinvent the wheel. All of our mobile creations are based on existing vehicles of different sizes, from trolleys to trailers and caravans, that we have reused as the base for each project. Start by stripping back a donor vehicle to its chassis and then constructing your new architectural proposal on top of the existing internal framework.

By utilizing the mass-produced and industrially engineered running gear, such as the wheels and braking system, you are free to concentrate your design-thinking on the actual architectural proposition rather than worry too much about suspension and drive shafts. An added bonus is that you can also be confident that the finished project will actually be ready for operation on the road.

Try to work as closely as you can with the people who will actually fabricate the project as early as possible in the design process. Or, even better, have a go at making it yourself! Tearing things apart is a good thing and seeing how the bits and pieces fit together helps you understand how they work as well as giving you further appreciation of the potential of materials and craftsmanship.

Don't Get a Job, <u>Make a Job</u>

Specialism vs diversity

Having a specialism, being unique, and putting all your eggs in a perfectly designed basket can be scary. However, as the world diversifies and our needs and wants vary, it becomes increasingly important to be able to offer something different. Pursuing your interests is always a good bet—if you like what you do, you're likely to do it well. The following specialist case studies have carved niche markets from a hectic design landscape. If you do something very specific and you do it well, you can quickly and easily become the go-to person for that task. Get focused. Be special.

However, Jack-of-all-trades, master-of-none is quite simply an archaic and inaccurate idiom. The rise in diversification has been paramount in the last decade, and to stay afloat many companies and individuals have "covered their bases" by providing more than one service and spreading risk. In times of economic uncertainty this is a valid business move; however, there are a number of driven individuals for whom this creative balance is just their way of life. The following diversifiers and specialists have used the wide range of skills learned in their design courses at university and applied them to a vast set of actionable projects.

Don't Get a Job, <u>Make a Job</u>

Strategy:

Don't be afraid to experiment

Le Creative Sweatshop

Stéphane Perrier, one third of French design collective Le Creative Sweatshop (LCSS)—the other two members being Julien Morin and Matieu Missiaen—says he has always known that their work was different and that, with their perpetual thirst for learning and finding new ways of doing things, LCSS's success is set to continue. Basing their work in the physical and dynamic world of volume, LCSS are specialists when it comes to materials and formal experimentation. They seek out the most unlikely materials to use in their personal projects as well as in their commissioned art direction for the likes of Nissan, Hermès, Stella McCartney, and Cartier. The team is committed to originality and quality; most pieces are handmade, which gives them a humble, precious, and fragile quality. As a dynamic, supple, and reactive agency, LCSS—with the help of their network of partners— enjoys success in making material innovations.

LCSS might not necessarily naturally identify themselves as "specialists", since they work in a variety of industries in different ways, but their approach to materiality is their unique selling point, the thread that holds their portfolio of work together, the trait that makes them stand out from the crowd. The sheer originality of the work produced is impressive—along with these high standards for innovation comes a lot of pressure. It takes guts putting this level of trust in a material you have never worked with before, but with hand-working these materials comes a certain amount of honesty and confidence in the product. Having friends around you and solid sources of inspiration are lifesavers in this kind of situation. Being a specialist does not have to mean a repetitive, one-track line of work— in fact, being a specialist can open the door of opportunity to very special places indeed.

Above and previous page: 5 Fruits
Opposite: Jimmy Fairley, French
sunglasses brand

Experience

When I was at school, my teachers didn't understand what I was trying to do with all these sculptures and 3-D renderings—there was an accepted way of doing things and they didn't think outside of these narrow confines. So when I finished school I searched for internships everywhere, and with a lot of luck my first internship turned into the job I still have now. If I hadn't been creative about my future I would probably be sitting in front of a computer in a communal office for graphic designers, and I can't stand that, so I'm happy to work on something different and real, not digital, pretty much every day.

We are a trio, we each bring something to the collective, and that's our strength. We support and motivate each other. I know a lot of friends who work at home and feel demotivated because there is no rhythm to the day—you are alone with your computer. For us, it's the opposite. We don't start early but when the day begins everyone has his/her work to do and by the end of the day it's unbelievable to see what we have accomplished!

With no particular design degrees between us, we have managed to work in several mediums using different techniques during the last five years. We are in our own school and we choose what we are trying to learn. We began in 2009 by crafting paper, and after that we felt the need to change medium and develop a more diverse range of materials. In the last four years we have worked with concrete, jelly, plastic, Plexiglas, and a lot more. Each time we change techniques, it's like starting a new class!

Advice

If we could say anything to the younger generation, it would be "Do what you like and don't listen to others". We tried a lot of things until we found something really original and that we really like. This job requires a lot of courage and patience but it's worth it, because every day you have to try something new with no boss around—just music, friends, and perseverance.

We don't really like receiving CVs by mail. We much prefer meeting people, seeing how they present their work, and whether they have the right craft skills. But it's hard to find someone who is really handy with a lot of techniques, so if we find someone who is interesting and motivated, we can teach him or her our ways of working and new techniques.

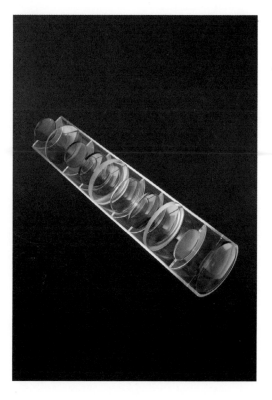

"We do a lot of experimentation and photograph the results almost every day to enhance our work."

Stéphane Perrier

Little Free Library

Strategy:

Learn from your idols

Stereotank

The route into specialism can be intentional—addressing a niche not catered for in the market—or accidental, following your instincts and desires and discovering naturally recurring themes.

Both of these were the case for New York-based architecture and design duo Marcelo Ertorteguy and Sara Valente, aka Stereotank. With independence being the ultimate goal, prior to forming Stereotank the pair separately sought out experience in similarly situated practices in order to learn the necessities of operating as a business within their chosen field. This is a smart move. Exposing yourself to the types of situations you are likely to encounter while being mentored by others is an excellent way to prepare for the eventualities of conducting business independently. It should not be looked upon as "spying", but as research, training, and groundwork. This also prepares you for the future, as one day these may be the same firms you will compete against for projects and clients.

From top: Cyclo-phone; Cargo Guitar; Heartbeat

Experience

We didn't deliberately choose specialism over diversification, it just happened naturally by starting to work with our favourite subjects. Objects, themes, and ideas started to recur, creating a body of work with a defined direction and a vision. This portfolio is what has made everything happen. Each one of the projects gave a hint to make possible the next; there is no better publicist that your own built work.

As designers and artists we are mostly attracted to the non-conventional; we like to reinvent the wheel over and over again. Going back to basics always offers an opportunity for new insights, ways of looking at old things anew, with a fresh eye.

Being independent is the ultimate desire. Even though schools work as a laboratory for the professional practice, they never give you the real sense of exposure needed to be independent. Investing the first few years out of school in a practice with similar interests to yours could be very beneficial for your professional career; in order to "kill your idols" you must know them well.

Collaborations are essential for professional growth; usually they are productive when team members complement each other, when each member offers what the others lack. Collaborations are also very positive when members with similar mindsets participate, having a healthy and

> "Specialization can be as broad as diversification, by choosing one path you 'limit' yourself to a whole set of possibilities."
>
> Stereotank

productive competition.

In our case, a collaboration was the opportunity to make our first project happen in New York. It was a collaboration on multiple levels. We teamed up with two other designers (combo colab) and together applied for a grant offered by the Department of Transportation of New York through a non-profit organization (Hester Street Collaborative) that presented our proposal, which became known as "Mall-terations". The installation, built in 2009 and in place for over two years, celebrated the history of immigration on the Lower East Side neighbourhood by portraying historic facts painted on the floor in parallel with railroad track graphics that evoked the old elevated tracks, while five colourful benches that rotated 360 degrees enlivened the park.

What happened next

Here in New York the majority of the job opportunities for architects are in high-end residential, commercial, boutique design, hospitality, and some infrastructure; few small studios are able to focus their practice on projects where art and creativity are at the base of the endeavours, making the opportunities to work in this field very limited. This was one of the reasons why we found ourselves in the position of creating our own niche in the design world.

Having gone down the traditional route for some time prior to finding our own path taught us two important lessons; on the one hand it gave us the opportunity to see the profession from a standpoint that we couldn't have had as recent graduates on our own, and on the other hand it made us demand more from ourselves, creating a greater necessity for independence. The more freedom you have, the better you can think, and the better you can think, the happier you are.

"It should not be looked upon as 'spying,' but as research, training, and groundwork."

Gem Barton

Mall-terations

Fashion For Concrete

Strategy:

Repeat, repeat, improve, repeat

Fabrice Le Nezet

Sometimes you just know! Designer and maker Fabrice knew that he would never be 100 percent satisfied by a traditional job and, rather than fighting that realization, he embraced it—he decided to get a freelance job that would feed him and also give him enough free time to focus on his own work.

Through years of refinement and design iteration, Fabrice established his own unique style. Having a trademark style can be seen as a drawback to some, suggesting that you are not able to fully let go of the design process and hand over to a client's wants. Fabrice disagrees, believing that, by developing a style that is instantly recognizable as you, *you* become instantly recognizable—well, we can all spot a Wes Anderson film from 1,000 paces can't we? When you are not afraid of doing the same things over and over, you are free to improve and develop. This iterative process is inherent in the world of design. Repetition can be a positive measure; Fabrice calls it his quest to extract the essence of his work.

"Being specialized doesn't mean doing the same thing forever."

Fabrice Le Nezet

Spring/Summer 2012

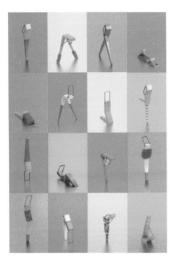

Experience

I have been working within a director collective for a few years now, producing very diverse work, from short films to music videos and TV commercials. We always try to explore different styles and push for every project to be a new experience. Our work has generally been very well received but sometimes we notice people struggle to picture our style easily and to recognize our work. When I started working on my own, I had no other goal than producing what I had in mind. However, project after project, I discover my approach to the creative process has completely changed.

Being specialized is a key point for me. By "specialized", I mean developing a unique style, something that everyone can recognize in my work. Every project you take on will advertise your work and your artist profile as a whole and create connections in people's minds. This way, you might potentially have people directly contacting you because they like what you do. The recurrent use of painted metal tubes and concrete volumes in my sculptural work is a trademark for me. Even though the concept behind the projects differs, the works can be easily linked.

By talking with other designers, I have discovered that many artists are doing far more diverse projects than you would expect. Generally they won't communicate on those projects, not because they don't like them but because they don't fit their image. So even if I have to or want to do very diverse things, I think it is important to ostensibly keep a clear profile.

Advice

It is useful to develop strong technical skills beside your artistic research—that way you will be able to easily find your first job. This might not be your dream job, but it will give you the financial independence to carry on your research. Paradoxically, the ideal job is the one that does not quite suit you 100 percent. Indeed, I would say ideas often come from frustration. Generally I get loads of new project ideas when I am stuck on some really boring job. Obviously finding the right balance isn't easy and is something you have to question all the time.

That said, I also think being able to adapt to different mediums is important. This can be an interesting way to renew and open your perspective.

Specializing doesn't mean having to do the same thing forever. You might get bored of it at some point or, even worse, you might get bored of your own work. Step by step, you can drive your style in new directions and, if you want to try something new, go ahead; with time you will find the connection. I started working on some toys, which developed into more minimalist and sculptural concrete toys, which finally ended up as actual concrete and metal sculptures.

"By developing a style that is instantly recognizable as you, *you* become instantly recognizable."

Gem Barton

Below: Measures: Weight
Bottom: Hurling Players

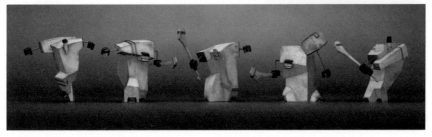

You And Me

Strategy:

Embrace the "busyness"

Adam Nathaniel Furman

Some people are born to juggle—they are at their happiest, most switched on, and inspired when multiple activities and connections are possible. Adam poetically refers to his multiple interests (architecture, design, making, and writing) as his "children", each running around independently, yet intrinsically connected. He says that he has no favourites and all make up the dynamic of the family as a whole.

Working in many areas is not always an efficient mode of practice; each takes time to nurture and master. Diversifiers are likely to find they spend much of their free time busying themselves with side projects and learning new techniques, but the possibilities these endeavours create are infinite.

Just like Adam, diversifiers have to be agile, nimble, proactive go-getters—they want it, they need it, and they make it happen! The ferocious appetite for success and ability to curate such a lifestyle are traits no client or potential employer can ignore.

"I did all of my work in the evenings, the early mornings, and the weekends; the quintessential geek on his own at the computer is just my way of working."

Adam Nathaniel Furman

Experience

I have found that I enjoy working on several things at the same time, and I find it difficult being without any one of them. It's a little like having a big family with lots of kids running around the place, juggling all their needs, and it being a bit hectic at times, but the household being full of love and joy because of it. So journalism, poetry, film, product design, art, interiors, architecture, and ceramics are all like the kids that I want to spend an equal amount of time with, and who play with each other, teaching each other the things that they learn and bring to the family individually.

It was virtually impossible for me to break into the world of design and media and publicity through a normal route—my stuff doesn't fit in well enough—so the Internet has been amazing. I could put my own work out there, and people found it and gave me the sense that it was worthwhile to carry on. Out in the blog world I found my own little audience, which eventually grew wider, and while it is still pretty niche, it has begun to catch the attention of a few teeny tiny corners of mainstream media. The Internet allowed me to do weird, complex, difficult work that still found an audience, without the need to dumb anything down for a "market".

I did all of my work in the evenings, the early mornings, and the weekends; the quintessential geek on his own at the computer is just my way of working. This obviously changes from project to project, as when I'm working on something architectural I collaborate much more, and with a broader range of people, and on products I work very closely with the makers, which is normally a chain of two or three companies and as many individuals. But I do like having a certain amount of space to myself so that I can explore ideas in a nonverbal way. This will change no doubt, or at least hopefully, if I am lucky enough and the scale of my projects increases …

What happened next

I didn't ditch the traditional route on purpose. I've always sent out my CV in the usual way, perhaps with less luck than others because my CV is odd: If I was looking for an architect to take care of a job, or a draftsman to be solid and follow a project, I would also look at my CV and think "What? How is he going to help?". So I ended up gaining employment through other means. For example, one employer was, unbeknownst to me, a follower of mine on Twitter, and she had gained an idea of what I do, how I think, and my range of skills from there and was keen to take me on. Another office that I had applied to many times before took me on after, again unbeknownst to me, someone who had taught me and who I had worked with and by coincidence had worked with the director of that office before, called him up and gave him the lowdown on me, and after the interview went really well, I was in. Then there are the things I have progressed into through competitive selection based on project proposals, like the Designers In Residence at the Design Museum, and the American Academy's Rome Prize, as well as being awarded an AA Research Cluster to Run. In these cases my skill at proposing intriguing briefs came to the fore, and I guess I romanced the juries into going for it, and luckily the pudding came out as good proof in each instance for further proposals in the future. Journalism was a great experience. I had always written a lot, and when blogs became popular I began writing a few of those, writing for free on friends' blogs, and when I recently needed some extra cash and sent out e-mails to a few magazine editors, I had a great back catalogue of online articles I could send to them for reference; a few of them liked what I had written and now I am writing for *The Architectural Review*, *RIBA Journal*, *Disegno*, and *T-r-e-m-o-r-s*.

Top to bottom: Folly Ring, Identity Parade, Complex

"Diversifiers have to be agile, nimble, proactive go-getters."

Gem Barton

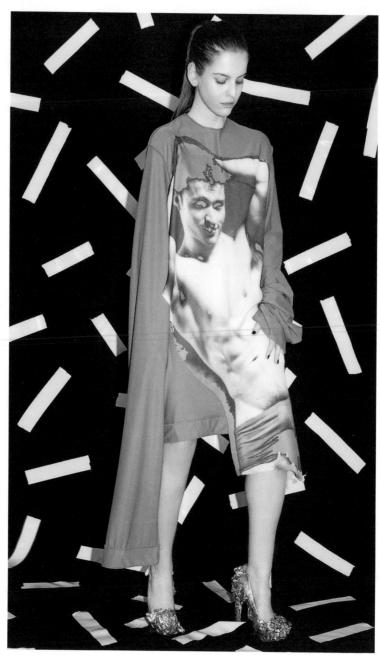

AW14 Conceptual Collection

Don't Get a Job, <u>Make a Job</u>

Strategy:

Swim against the tide

Vin & Omi

With qualifications in geography and anthropology and a portfolio of projects covering public art, consultation, fashion design, and art directing, talented duo Vin & Omi (Kevin Wilson and Omi Ong) have experience of almost everything creative and have applied their skills to all of these industries successfully. An awareness and realistic view of the different modes of business plays a large part in their decision-making; being creative and being business-minded are not mutually exclusive, as many of the case studies in this book demonstrate.

Vin & Omi have independently and collectively: run large public arts organizations, designed latex garments, worked with A-list celebrities, project managed, and consulted on renowned design projects and masterplans. In order to move seamlessly between varied disciplines you need to be agile, flexible, organized, and hungry.

"An awareness and realistic view of the different modes of business are important."

Gem Barton

Above: AW14
Opposite, left: Chrome Collection,
Right: Moth Collection

Experience

We have made a point of NOT following the traditional two-fashion-collections-a-year normal progression of a fashion brand. We act as consultants to the industry and have developed accessories, menswear, and a diffusion line before we launched our main brand. This gives us a range of revenue streams and a strong portfolio of work.

Although set up primarily as a fashion label, Vin & Omi, we soon decided that the traditional way of showing fashion wasn't for us. The seasonal production of collections is fraught with difficulty and the system of producing fashion in this way produces strains on cash flow and creativity. We decided that focusing only on fashion would not work for us and decided a multi-design process would work. We cross lots of design platforms, directing music videos as well as making public art. We keep ourselves flexible and fluid creatively, and sail hard against traditional fashion models.

We are very sure of our vision and, as a long-term partnership, we have developed a way of discussing our creative ideas. We are not interested in pleasing a fashion audience in terms of fitting into trends or colours—we work outside of the fashion machine. We have found the fashion industry restrictive and that support is biased toward friends of friends and is heavy on networking. We moved our studio to the Cotswolds in the English countryside to avoid the networking machine and concentrate on what we wanted to do. We collaborate with many other organizations and also act as consultants; we are firm believers that creative brains can do anything creative.

We have purposely honed a wide range of skills between us. We are both artists and marketeers, we design and construct garments. Each of us is computer savvy. We are both paid to consult for other brands and creatives. For some shoots we do the photography, hair and makeup, and we also direct and edit our own and others' videos.

Advice

For us, going alone was the only option, as we can do what we like, when we like—you cannot put a price on self-sufficiency. One thing we would say is that if either one of us had tried to do this solo it would not have worked, so for us finding a partner was crucial.

It's easier to meet clients if you are social animals, which we were. You then have a ready-made list of guinea pigs for your clothes. Then slowly we built up a client list. Some designers are flagrant networkers and really push social media to the max. We are a little more discreet and I think some of our more successful clients appreciate this.

Lastly, we make sure that we keep a diverse portfolio of projects on the go to keep us financially viable. We need to for the business model we run.

"Look at what everyone else is doing and go the other way—seriously. There are too many people following the same path. You are creative—swim the other way."

Kevin Wilson

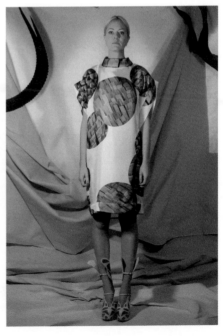

NCCA Moscow concept collage

Don't Get a Job, <u>Make a Job</u>

Strategy:

Question everything

WAI Architecture Think Tank

Practice imitates life—if as individuals you are interested in multiple creative areas, let this also be the model for your professional development. Cruz Garcia and Nathalie Frankowski are in equal portions WAI Architecture Think Tank, Garcia Frankowski Art Practice, and Intelligentsia Gallery—they develop their projects as architects, authors, curators, gallerists, designers, and public speakers, but most importantly as people. Each platform is founded with a desire to take risks and do things differently. In identifying an opportunity the pair waste no time and forge forward with their unique approach to addressing the need.

Each project they pursue is based on a strong sense of responsibility and commitment. When trying to develop innovative ways to challenge the status quo you will inevitably become familiar with having to take risks. Faced with this need daily, Cruz and Nathalie have developed the ability to question everything: education, professional life, disciplinary commitment, and the role of intellectual rigour in the creation and understanding of art and architecture.

Committing themselves fully to more than one venture could have been a difficult balance for the duo. But they have managed to cleverly overlap their focus, their jobs, and their passions to the point where, while the medium may differ greatly, their message does not—innovate, experiment, question everything.

Experience

After we met in 2008 in Brussels, we quickly realized that the current state of architecture (and life, for that matter) was not what we expected. In order to address this problem we decided to create our own platform. WAI Architecture Think Tank was devised as a stage that could provide us with the freedom to take risks and think for ourselves. Through WAI we developed a space where publishing, theory, research, book making, architecture, and urban design were fuelled by an authentic sense of intellectual curiosity and hunger for criticality. WAI offered a screen onto which we could project our intentions, goals, and aspirations. It allowed us to pursue an alternative architectural practice.

Following the creation of WAI Think Tank we developed a parallel art practice named Garcia Frankowski. This operation allowed us to pursue interests that are not necessarily related to architecture, so in a way it provided us with a channel to address other forms of fundamental questioning. On that same note, in January 2014 we co-founded a concept-driven curatorial and exhibition space for contemporary art in Beijing. Intelligentsia Gallery was created to challenge an art scene dominated by vague economic forces, and provided space for truly international and intellectually rigorous exhibitions presenting the work of artists from around the world in an environment where art, artists, intellectuals, and the public are invited to rethink the relationship between art and life, concepts and creation. Intelligentsia Gallery, Garcia Frankowski, and WAI Architecture Think Tank are diverse platforms

NCCA Moscow promenade montage

that invite us to address universal questions about art, society, architecture, and our physical and ideological environment.

Ludwig Wittgenstein affirmed that the limits of your language mean the limits of your world. We aim to create different tools that allow us to communicate with a diversified disciplinary vocabulary (an architectural vocabulary, an art vocabulary, and an intellectual vocabulary) in order to expand our world, and critique the world.

Advice

Artists should work for what they believe in, they should pursue their interests, they should look for answers to their questions, and they should create tools to answer these questions. As a result, the image of the work, and the image of the artist, should reflect the values he stands for, not in a moralistic sense but in the sense of pursuing freedom in the arts and making our lives better in the realm of architecture. That would be success in our eyes, to be able to create work that reflects our values. If you're only successful by altering your values, if you respond blindly to the requests and demands of an unfair infrastructure of power, then we wouldn't be interested in that type of success. We're only interested in one type of success, and that success lies within fulfilling your own expectations without compromising your values.

Pure Hardcore Icons:
Sphere City and Pyramid City

"Innovate, experiment, question everything."

WAI Architecture Think Tank

Be T-shaped

Advice on specialism and diversity from Jason Bruges,
Jason Bruges Studio

It is about depth of knowledge: specialists have a depth of knowledge in one area. The studio here is full of specialists, however quite often that depth will be crossed with another broad skill. For example, some of the hybrids we have here within the team include architecture crossed with interaction design, architecture crossed with set design, and architecture crossed with landscape design. Also, specialism would seem to dictate a narrow marketplace, however ours is again quite broad as the narrow specialist skills can be applied to many different areas: film, branding, events, retail, development, visitor experience, and so on.

It is important to have a variety of designers, both specialists and diversifiers, in the world of design. It is a way of people being able to compete. The great thing about specialisms is they can be invented. The cross between digital environment and architecture didn't really exist 20 years ago.

My interest in digital design comes a little from the route I took academically, but also from being exposed to technology when I was younger. My father built and designed computer systems, so from an early age I was exposed to a mix of technology and art. I would build interventions at home that would track occupancy—I remember building a sensitive staircase when I was about eight or nine out of springs and foil and wires!

When I studied architecture at Oxford Brookes University I was interested in high tech and also the intelligence of buildings. I had tuition from people who were pushing boundaries in environmental design, environmental psychology, cladding design, and space architecture. I created a performance installation in my final year which represented a piece of music in light and material, and a performance space that turned the tables on the audience. At the Bartlett School of Architecture I spent time in the "Interactive Architecture Lab", which was Unit 14 under Stephen Gage and Pete Silver, designing, creating, making, testing, iterating, and thinking about experimental, interactive, responsive, performative digital architecture. This led to me making a series of architectural art installations using a mixed-media digital palette which has acted as the springboard for what I am practising/creating within the JBS studio environment.

Some specialists might be one-trick-ponies. However, I think a lot of specialists have to be "T-shaped"—broad and with depth as generalizing specialists. I think specializing takes a lot of skill as you have to learn a base and then another skill on top of that. You may be inventing a new profession with new rules too—very exciting, but daunting at the same time

Anyone wanting to specialize shouldn't try to preempt it. Follow your instincts of what you think you will be interested in and specialism will happen along the way. Being multidisciplinary often comes through being a part of a team, which is going to come naturally for most architectural/construction- and design-related disciplines. University courses give lots of natural breaks for specialism whether through units, subject groups, higher levels of study, etc.

Don't be scared of diversifying as a company or as an individual. You will quite often have very interesting insights as a skilled newcomer to a sector or professional discipline that mean you arrive at novel ways of doing things. We have competed on many projects where we may be working on visitor experience, exhibition design, lighting/feature design, and set design. While these are not our key disciplines as architects and design engineers, through curiosity and rigour, and through the studio's design philosophy, we arrive at innovative and original ways of looking at the world, and this is inherently interesting and very marketable.

Don't Get a Job, <u>Make a Job</u>

Tough calls

Everybody will, at some point, question their progress, their process, and their reasons for being and doing. Each and every person featured in this book—designer, academic, and student—will have faced a difficult decision with a potentially life-changing impact. More often than not this difficult situation becomes a catalyst or motivator for the future. When times are tough, we see the importance in evaluating our goals. This refocusing is a very important part of keeping on track and developing as a person and a designer.

The following featured designers have had to make tough, life-changing decisions early in their careers. This can be daunting, but by weighing up your options and balancing them with your personal checklist for a happy design career, making these tough calls can be the making of you.

Strategy:

Trust your instincts

Jose Garrido

Having the conviction to trust your instincts is an extremely valuable quality to possess at any age. While still at design school, (now) art director and designer Jose Garrido saw the value in working on competition briefs for real clients in his spare time, and fought hard to be allowed to do so during class time too. Submitting proposals to competitions immediately increases the visibility of you and your work, which may be seen by renowned industry professionals on judging panels, by clients themselves, and, if conducted well, may be picked up by design blogs and websites with thousands of hits per day. Working to competition briefs shows a dedication to your industry, responsibility, focus, and the ability to search out work, follow a brief, and keep to deadlines. Being able to talk about well-known brands in a job interview, rather than about generic unnamed student projects, can make for a better flow of conversation and an authentic connection.

Jose decided to leave education, but this kind of decision should not be taken lightly. Jose considered all of his options seriously, spoke at length with his family, and decided to take the risk. He was already receiving acclaim for the work he had done, and was being offered the kinds of commission he had once only dreamed of getting after graduation. Getting a head start was the right thing to do for Jose, but it was a risk nevertheless. Every decision we make is a calculated risk, with different odds. You should give your decision the correct amount of consideration, follow your heart, and always have a back-up plan.

OK COURT VICTORY PUMP II
ate: 1987   White/Purple/Blood orange

REEBOK - CANTON, MASSACHUSETTS, USA

Sneaker Coolture project

"Leaving my degree was a difficult decision, mainly because I wanted to finish it and make my mother proud, but in the end it was the best option, and she understood that. Now she is really proud to see me getting nice jobs and doing what I love."

Jose Garrido

Experience

It all began when I was selected as an Honourable Mention in the Behance (online platform for showcasing creative work) Student Showdown design competition (2012) with my AVANTH typeface project. I was lucky enough to be chosen along with five other students from more than 1,200 submissions. My work began to be seen on lots of sites and I was contacted by a creative agency in Florida to work freelance for them.

I have always thought that real projects motivate students much more than hypothetical academic exercises. Just swap the brand "x" in a school assignment for a real brand and you will see how students work harder. Even more so if it is for an actual potential client. I guess that you always aspire to get your work seen in real life, and not just in your class.

When I was in my second year, I saw that a packaging contest was being held by a US brand. I told one of my tutors about it and finally convinced her to set an assignment for it. I ended up doing my best work and was selected as a finalist for my EOS Coffee packaging. After that, lots of publishers contacted me, asking to feature the project in design books. All this from a project used as a school assignment!

What happened next

Early last year, I started contacting a lot of different magazines to ask them if they needed some work. One day I saw that a design studio in New York was looking for a graphic designer and I wrote them an e-mail. They liked my work and I started working with them on some branding projects. My first big client was Gatorade, with whom I collaborated on some typography compositions. At that time I was mostly exploring lettering- and typography-based works that were appealing to certain kinds of client. I came up with a collection project with some recent lettering artworks, which was featured on Behance and then spread through lots of inspiration sites. I suppose people from the Nike team saw them and they contacted me last May to make two T-shirts.

Above: Nike competition final design and concept image
Below: EOS Coffee packaging

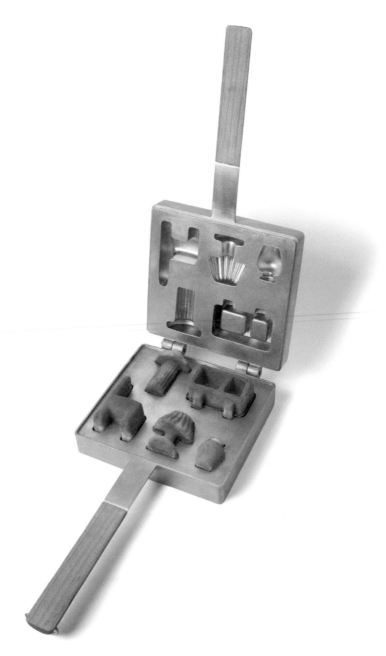

Sapore Dei Mobili

Strategy:

Move mountains

Rui Pereira

Sometimes, in order to have a chance of achieving your goals, you need to make sacrifices. Designer Rui relocated numerous times in order to chase his dreams, gaining knowledge and insight, with the goal of experiencing multiple cultures and realities. This enables him to design conscious and relevant products. Moving countries is not something we are all necessarily able to do, but, for Rui, being exposed to different societies was of paramount importance to his personal development as a designer. For him, this was a must, and when you feel this passionately about something, sometimes you have to move mountains to make it happen.

Whether you toil over the benefits and drawbacks of such difficult decisions, or whether you follow your gut instinct and allow spontaneity to take over—quite often the biggest risks reap the biggest rewards, financial or otherwise.

"Designers have to experience different realities and ways of working until they are ready to design conscious products that are relevant to the consumer."

Rui Pereira

Experience

I'd always wanted to start my own studio and fully focus on my work. However, in Portugal (my home country), the industry doesn't recognize the value of young designers. After struggling for 18 months to get some commissions, I decided to move to Milan, Italy. After I finished a double master's in product and interior design, I did a three-month internship at an interior design studio, which was extended for a year and a half. I made the most of the design scene in Milan and started developing my personal projects while working a full-time job. Building a portfolio that could show my full potential allowed me to get a better job later on.

When I left university, I only had a few creative tools to my name and no clue of how the design industry worked. It was (and still is) very important to me to work for others, in order to understand how the industry works from the inside, how to deal with clients and suppliers, and how to manage a studio in the best way.

I aim to create an immediate connection between user and object using a clear language with a humorous twist. My research focuses on finding new perspectives and experiences, while creating new typologies. In Milan I had the opportunity to work with top Italian manufacturers and experience many production techniques and environments. Once I had finally achieved a good position within the design team and could work at the level I fought for, I decided I needed to see another side of the industry. Until this point, I had been more involved in the creative process, but I felt I could

Sapore Dei Mobili

improve my technical knowledge if I worked closer to the manufacturers. These thoughts started to materialize and I searched for a new job, this time in Scandinavia, to which I always felt a special connection design-wise. A few months ago I got a job at a furniture company and moved from Italy to Denmark. This cultural shock is providing me with plenty of material for new projects: Even if this change is quite recent it feels like I've taken the right step. In my opinion, designers have to experience different realities and ways of working until they are ready to design conscious products that are relevant to the consumer.

Throughout the years I've met several colleagues who shared the same work philosophy, which has led to several collaborations. I feel that the results are stronger when you exchange ideas with others. The different cultural backgrounds always bring something new to the table. A lot of the time something you take for granted is a surprise to others, and this can even be the start of a new project.

> "When you feel this passionately about something, sometimes you have to move mountains to make it happen."
>
> Gem Barton

Advice

My advice to new designers is to always be alert to what surrounds you, work for others before you start your own studio, and be very patient.

I think, if you want to work in creative fields, you have to love what you do and fight everyday for it. Try to find your own path and understand how to build your identity and create a space for yourself within the industry. I always knew I would not be completely satisfied with my professional life if I stopped working on my personal projects. That's the main reason why I always kept doing external collaborations and exhibits while working for somebody else. This way I could financially support myself while learning how to structure my own studio from the knowledge I gained from the people I work for.

Build best-case scenarios in your imagination

Advice on facing tough calls from Jimenez Lai, Bureau Spectacular

One of my favourite thought exercises is the projection of multiple futures. It is about revisiting your personal past and constructing branches of five, six, or seven possible futures. What decisions have I made in my life that have led up to this moment? This thought crosses my mind during moments of intense trouble or pleasure. If every fork in the road leads to either a path of happiness or one of regret, it is comforting to remind ourselves that alternate timelines exist. No matter what we choose, a future on the other side of that fork in the road happened. That reality exists—it is just not ours. There is no sense in stewing in regret because your best hopes and wishes exist in that other world out there.

With this knowledge in mind, we can preemptively construct these plural paths. Is it possible to open an exhibition next year? Can I be friends with these people I admire? Will I move to a city of my liking, working in exactly the ways I would otherwise envy? The answer is always yes to every possible future. If you have the courage to build a best-case scenario timeline in your imagination, that reality is already as good as real.

I lived in a desert shelter at Taliesin, Arizona, in 2004, and resided in a shipping container on the piers of Rotterdam at Atelier Van Lieshout in 2005. During those years, my relationship with material goods transformed, as I realized I did not need many of the societal norms I was brought up to "need". I subsequently began intensely compartmentalizing my life, reducing all that is personal to an extremely low proportion, and spent the majority of my time in production mode. I published my first book entitled *Citizens of No Place* with Princeton Architectural Press in 2012. In 2014, I was the designer and curator for the Taiwan Pavilion at the Venice Architecture Biennale. I also had the great pleasure of being in the permanent collection at the Museum of Modern Art with my installation work *White Elephant*, and seven of my accompanying drawings for that project. I am currently a professor at the school of architecture at UCLA.

Many of my first projects were self-initiated. Nobody commissioned me at the beginning. I subscribed to the "if you build it, they will come" business model instead of the "show me the money" train of thought. I felt that I needed some years of building up a strong argument about why I like what I like, and in that way I would not need to compromise my time and efforts. To begin, I was able to sustain my life and my work by teaching at universities and getting grants.

My advice is: write a few "fake" CVs for versions of your future selves—craft them, let your ambition run wild, project a few futures. No one is watching and there is no sense in feeling ashamed about these fake futures. I promise you, as you print them out and hold your plural futures in your hands, you will gain a deep sense of clarity about what you want to do and what you do not care to do.

Don't Get a Job, <u>Make a Job</u>

Going it alone vs teaming up

After years of instruction, direction, rules, and regulations at college or university, for many the thought of being your own boss, making your own decisions/mistakes, and taking charge of your own future may be preferable.

Barriers to entry into the creative industries have never been so low. This means entering this market as a new graduate can be smooth, which is a great thing for young entrepreneurs and collaborative groups. In order to take that step, it is important to carefully consider your options, but at some point the thinking has to stop and the doing has to start. Be smart about things, but don't let worries of profit margins and contracts stop you before you have started.

But what about the risks involved? Could teaming up with like-minded individuals be an option? There can be strength in numbers, feelings of warmth and support, bubbling excitement from being deep inside the hubbub—a sense that together you can achieve anything.

The following case studies illustrate the full breadth of the spectrum, from one-man bands to free-form collectives.

#084/2/2 Hip Flask

Strategy:

Think "original"

Tom Cecil

Tom left a well-paid job and good promotion prospects as an engineer at a well-known architecture practice to make things in his brother's garden. To many this might sound drastic, but Tom was unhappy in his daily routine working for someone else, so one day he decided to go it alone. He began by going part-time, allowing him the security he would need to experiment, and experiment he did, with different materials, techniques, and strategies as he attempted to discover what type of designer he was.

Many people daydream at work of all the other things they would rather be doing, but Tom took the leap and he now works successfully for himself, making bespoke pieces of furniture and as a specialist fabricator. Such a transition should not be considered an easy option; it will likely take its toll, and striding out alone is not for the faint-hearted. Tom was wise to phase his move into self-employment; this can reduce financial risk and minimize the cultural shock one can face when switching from a nine-to-five routine and embarking on a more free-form process.

"I knew that I wanted a studio where I made all the decisions about how it was set up, run and occupied. I knew it was going to be stressful, but it was my only choice ..."

Tom Cecil

#218 Sofa

Experience

I had a really good job and career ahead of me in engineering the acoustics of buildings, but I was always daydreaming about things I wanted to make: buildings, furniture, installations, products. I couldn't bear the thought of wasting all this time doing something I no longer cared for, and talk of promotion caused a cold sweat.

I went part-time as a consultant and started making furniture in the garden of my brother's house, experimenting with the materials and forms I'd always found interesting. It was a bit like sending myself to school or art college. I didn't even know what I wanted to be so I began making products, art installations, and learning new techniques—it was a really creative time.

Sometime in 2008 I went to an exhibition at a gallery and at the suggestion of my then-girlfriend I nervously went to speak to the gallerist and introduced myself, explaining what I did. They liked my work, and in March 2009 I installed a prototype of my #033 Steel rope bench at a pop-up they held in Clerkenwell, London. It didn't go anywhere then but I still hope to build it one day.

In the first two years I experimented a lot and widely; welding, woodworking, casting concrete, making ice sculptures, melting glass, casting metal—I was trying to figure out what I was and where I sat among my peers. I didn't know how

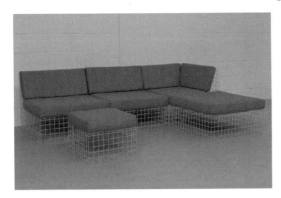

to introduce myself to people—what do you do? I didn't make much money but I really felt it was important to figure out what I was all about. It wasn't always a very easy or happy time, but I feel I know myself now, and I didn't before.

Advice

I think that if you're going to do something, you should do it really well. There are enough people who just want to fudge it and get by. When I'm making metalwork for artists I'll ask what style of welding do they want, which often gets the response "Um, what do you mean?" No one's ever offered them that before. They come to the workshop, and I'll weld using a few different techniques, which can really change the aesthetic of the piece. It might be subtle but hugely important for the artist. By knowing and understanding more, I can offer something unique.

Reflect a lot on what you are doing and if it really is where you want to be going. Don't be afraid to change your mind, or to stop if it's not working out well and try something new. Challenge what people tell you. It might be right, but you need to be sure in yourself that it is. You have to be true to yourself, though that might not make you instantly successful. Success is related to lots of different things but you have to be honest and be yourself. Whether people like it or not is out of your control. If other people do like and want to buy it that's great—but you have to have your own identity.

It might seem like a huge challenge in a world so saturated by visual culture, but original thinking and putting it into practice is hugely valuable in the long run, even if it takes ages. You do see people design things to get people's attention or to be popular and I think that's wrong—you should create things that reflect you.

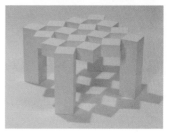

#146 Auxetic table

"Many people daydream at work of all the other things they would rather be doing …"

Gem Barton

Lumino City

Strategy:

Don't run before you can walk

State of Play

Like many other ambitious young creatives, Luke Whittaker was unfulfilled by his post-university work experiences. While happy to climb the ladder slowly, Luke wanted more control over his own career, so he leapt into the world of freelancing and has never looked back.

He entered the world of videogame design during a time of economic downturn. Even potential investors questioned his timing, but this was not something that concerned Luke, perhaps because the videogames industry is one that has continued to grow regardless. Being aware of the world around you, and understanding your chosen market and your position within it, is key to surviving. Being a sole trader with minimal overheads can be a big plus here—you can react quickly to changing tides, free of the restraining costs and worries associated with running a large firm.

Early growth as an individual or small company is of course important, but growing too fast, taking on too many jobs, contributors, and commitments can be very dangerous. As incoming fees and payments may be staggered and sporadic, while outgoings are regular and expanding, many young firms that grow too fast can find themselves in trouble financially. Be aware of your trajectory, choose your projects carefully (it is OK to turn down inappropriate work), and don't run before you can walk.

Luke remains focused on his early decisions. He continues to enjoy being independent and not answering to others, and steers clear of hierarchical structures that can be damaging to development and happiness.

"… I knew it was a gamble but I'd had requests coming in for work."

Luke Whittaker

Top: A Break in the Road
Above: Lumino City

Experience

While at university I did work experience as a runner for a special effects company in Soho, thinking that I loved animation and films, but I discovered that it had inherited the structure of the film and TV industry. You needed to prove yourself for years at the bottom before anyone would let you do anything interesting. I remember being asked to leave a room by a senior producer because I was showing an interest in an animator's work. I felt that the hierarchy strangled any creativity and fun.

I was fortunate to get my first job at a web-design company that was a little understaffed, which meant I had to do a lot myself. I learned to program and be self-sufficient, and within a year I went freelance. Some of my university work had been noticed, and that helped give me a boost.

Deciding to go it alone didn't seem like a tough decision at all—I knew it was a gamble but I'd had requests coming in for work while I was still employed in my first job, so felt reasonably confident that there was work out there. I made sure I saved about three months' wages and then gave myself the challenge of seeing if it would get off the ground within that time.

My university work, A Break in the Road, won a couple of awards. I put it on the Internet for people to play for free and suddenly it went everywhere, with people e-mailing it to friends as this was before Facebook and Twitter. I ended up with a huge bill from my hosting company as I'd gone over my limit, so my first success was also a financial disaster! But it did get the work in front of thousands, and clients got in touch; I created a whole new version for Shockwave, and MTV asked me to make a music-based game for them and I could make what I wanted and name a budget. At the time it seemed like the dream job, but now we invest our own money into the games, which is a little more risky but gives us even more control.

I freelanced for five years, occasionally working with a programmer or sound designer. I can do both, but I've learned not to take on too much: I'm an artist mainly, and other people are often far more qualified at the other disciplines. In 2008, I set up State of Play with my wife, which meant that we had a structure to employ others and create something bigger than just me. In the end there's only a certain amount that you can do yourself, especially with games that demand such a great amount of technical and artistic integration.

Initially we worked on smaller projects, giving us a large amount of creative control. There are huge triple-A videogames being made out there, but if you work for those companies you're likely only doing a small part of a large project. Being independent allowed us to explore and develop our own style, with our own ideas, and not need to fit to anyone else's plans.

Advice

I think having a great project that you can show to people when you graduate is massively important, or a body of good work plus a good website to show it off professionally. The website doesn't need to be complicated, just clear and simple.

I would recommend giving yourself a financial cushion of a few months if you can, as it means that you're starting under less pressure, which is good for your state of mind and probably helps you to assess where you're going more clearly. If you need to team up, it's a good idea to get an agreement in writing if possible, then everyone knows what's expected.

I didn't have a firm business plan, and still don't, only a conviction to keep doing better work and keep the spirit of creativity alive. You can't predict exactly what will happen in the business world, but you can guide yourself through the changes with a sense of purpose. For example, we were making Web games in 2009, but in 2010 the iPad came out and completely changed things—nobody knew if that would be a success or a failure. But it's given us even more creative freedom, even more control over publishing, and allowed us to create bigger and better projects. If we had had a business plan in 2009 we'd have had to rip it up!

If you can make the conditions right and not tie yourself to too many other pressures, then following your nose and intuition can be really rewarding. It's pretty much what being creative is all about.

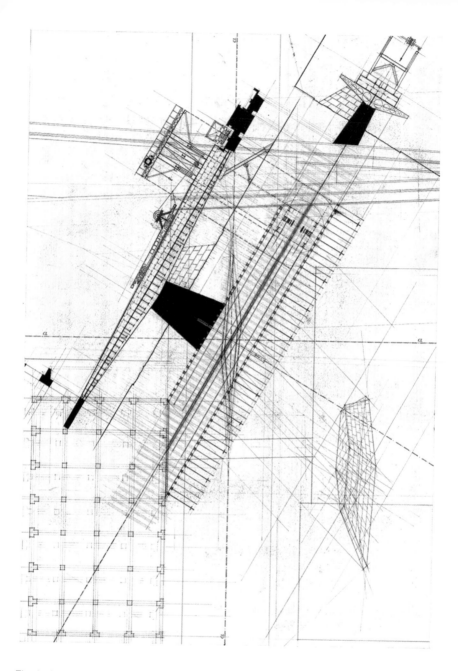

Thesis drawing

Don't Get a Job, <u>Make a Job</u>

Strategy:

Exploit your skills and interests
The Draftery

Jesen Tanadi successfully turned his hobby into a publishing platform accessed by tens of thousands of creatives every year, which hosts work from internationally acclaimed architects and designers and is one of the go-to inspiration sites for architecture students around the globe.

Through interning during summer vacations, Jesen realized that practising architecture was not what he had imagined, as he wanted to be involved with the entirety of a project rather than just a small part of the process. So instead he began to focus on the thing that really interested him about his architecture course: drawing. He began collecting images for his own reference, then shared them with his classmates and eventually founded The Draftery.

Going it alone is not always a planned and conscious pathway; sometimes things fall into place and you jump on those opportunities before they pass. Jesen did just that; he worked hard, and didn't give in when he realized what he had worked so hard for at university was not what he had hoped. He turned a potentially demoralizing realization into the opportunity that he needed. As his project gained momentum he enlisted talented friends and teachers to help in his quest for sharing and publishing enticing architectural drawings.

"As long as you're committed to the work and willing to work hard toward a goal, no obstacle is too great."

Jesen Tanadi

Experience

I studied architecture at the Rhode Island School of Design, a place where non-normative approaches to architecture were encouraged. The work I enjoyed making sat comfortably within the tradition of paper architecture.

I spent my winters and summers interning at a handful of small firms in Providence, RI, and Boston, MA, expecting that I would enjoy professional practice. Unfortunately, I was disillusioned when I realized that 90 percent of architectural practice wildly differed to what I had expected. I found that construction was too removed: most of the time, the things that you work on are only ideas and instructions that are executed by someone else—a set of legal documents tied up with the bureaucracy of building. The more I worked in architecture, the more my school work began to stray away from reality, which was reflected in the drawings I produced for my thesis.

After I graduated, I was wary of returning to professional practice. I knew that this wasn't what I wanted to do out of college. Instead of forcing myself to look for work in architecture, I decided to spend my time working on printmaking and graphic design—a couple of things I was interested in, but hadn't had the time to work on in school.

I stayed in Providence, looked for other ways to sustain myself, and tried to sort out what it was that I wanted to do. To kill time and keep the momentum going, I became a member at a local print shop and continued to expand on some of the printmaking skills I had picked up at college. I eventually became a key member, instructor, and contract printer there. However, I still had an interest in architecture, especially in architectural drawing. That summer I founded The Draftery, a platform that showcases exciting architectural drawings. It began as a blog-like website, a place where I could share a number of drawings I had been collecting. A couple of months into the project, I was contacted by a friend who had been working for a small publishing house in Tokyo, Japan, and The Draftery's printed publication series, *Figures*, was born.

At that point I had very little knowledge of what goes into a publication, so I invited Athan Geolas, a classmate from college, and Thomas Gardner, one of my professors at RISD, to help me work on the first publication. Athan has since become a permanent fixture at The Draftery, and Thomas still serves as our Advising Editor. By the second publication, I knew that I was interested in graphic design and was beginning to seriously consider graduate school. Over the next two years, while I applied to graduate schools, I continued to work on The Draftery.

The Draftery, *Fig. 01*

Advice

I've read a lot of books and articles that tell you to do what you love, to trust your instincts, and so on. While all of these things are true and important, those books and articles tend to forget the fact that you have to somehow support yourself while doing the things you love, especially at the beginning of your career. Get a day job.

Hard work and commitment beat almost any other traits. As long as you're committed to the work and willing to work hard toward a goal, no obstacle is too great. I've found that to get anywhere in the world of art/design/architecture, you need to be proactive, especially early on in your career. Very rarely will someone ask you out of the blue to be part of a show or to design something, so it's part of your job to be able to put your name out there.

The Draftery, Web

Don't become a hermit

Advice on going it alone from Tomas Klassnik,
The Klassnik Corporation

Going it alone? No fixed hours. No one stealing your mug. No boss! Setting up by yourself sounds great, but don't be too hasty ... unless you're reading this in a field of four-leaf clovers or already have a generous trust fund, in which case, what have you been waiting for?!

Getting a diversity of experience matters, particularly if you're going solo. Picking up a range of industry expertise (even the boring stuff) is essential in the long run. Coming into contact with what happens at all stages and scales of a variety of design projects will be good experience when you become the Swiss Army Knife of responsibilities of your own.

Working with small practices, whose critical thinking and approach to exploring the potential of design through writing, sculpture, installations, and the occasional building, taught me that often the most interesting architectural discourse is pursued through means beyond bricks and mortar: this was something that would be fundamental to the early stages of my career, when the only masonry I was using was transforming a brick into a hat. Detailing skyscrapers for a large practice didn't directly translate into my own first works but it did build an understanding of the profession's technical processes and protocols, which would prove useful to even the smallest job—and when the call comes to design that skyscraper, I'll be ready.

OK, so you've learned enough and are ready to get your own office stationery printed. You'll need a name ... but who are you? That name will define what others think you do, so don't think about who you are now but what you want to become. You'll also want to stand out. Surrounded by a swarm of acronyms and bored at the prospect of becoming a familiar MyNameHere Architects or Buzzword Studio, I chose to become a corporation! I wanted (and suspected I might have to) design more than just buildings, and no one is quite sure what a Corporation does. Also, the Klassnik Corporation sounded large, and when it comes to architecture, that's a good thing. People trust large organizations; they have due diligence officers and well-stocked stationery cupboards.

As an architect it can be particularly difficult to get going by yourself. Architecture is big and expensive and people like to know that the person designing their big and expensive thing knows what they're doing or, even better, has done it before! But whatever discipline you're going alone in, the most important thing is to start doing stuff. Any stuff. This will help you build your identity and discover what it is that you (yes, you, not your boss or colleagues) believe in. Agility and versatility are both necessities and advantages of going it alone. I started designing exhibitions, pop-up shops, speculating on cities of the future for fashion magazines, even hosting a séance to contact the spirit of Le Corbusier before the extensions, offices, galleries, landmarks, and public realm design work came along. Every project helps to define what you believe in while also building new audiences and future clients along the way.

Don't become a hermit. You may have chosen to go it alone but in fact networking outside the workplace will now become even more important. Look for arenas to continue critical dialogues to test your ideas; this may be exhibiting work, writing for magazines, or discussing the latest outrage on Twitter. Working part time and teaching helped to provide me with these essential conversations while also easing the financially daunting transition from the day job.

At some point, if you've followed this advice diligently, the work will be rolling in and you'll have to take the tough decision to recruit. Know what you're best at and find others to help you with the rest. Going it alone can be great but isn't necessarily meant to last forever. The world always needs new voices. Do you have something different to say? Are you ready to challenge the status quo? Then stay far away from timid. Only make moves when your heart's in it, and live the phrase "the sky's the limit".

New Hing Loon

Don't Get a Job, <u>Make a Job</u>

Strategy:

Even within a team, you need to be individual

Seán & Stephen Ltd.

Seán and Stephen ARE the business. If you hire them, you will work with them. Sometimes it is this simple. You start a business with someone because you admire them, and when you put together two distinct characters who genuinely work well as a team—it makes sense!

In joining forces, each of the pair is able to sustain their own creative satisfaction and walk the boundaries of architecture and design. There is an integral plurality in the business, benefiting the spirit and ability of the studio but at the same time navigating around deadlock conflicts of opinion—which can be heightened in times of pressure.

Ensuring individual personalities remain visible through the company's projects and manifesto is very important. Seán and Stephen don't wish to impose a homogenous or compromised design style—instead their company provides them with a framework to pursue their own individual interests and support each other in the process.

Experience

Some time ago, while studying, I [Seán] realized that peripheries are just as important as centres. This outward gaze manifested in 2011 when I resigned from a large-scale corporate architecture practice and eventually took a job at an interactive design house, designing and fabricating the set of a BBC TV ad. I went from planning airport passenger routes to designing for the TV camera with directors and producers. I experienced a wake-up call at that moment, realizing that I was not shocked or fazed by the industry and environment shift. I began to seriously question the prescribed framework of becoming an architect.

In August 2012 Stephen and I were both told by our respective bosses that we'd have to find other jobs. Only a few weeks later, when Stephen asked if I wished to enter a competition with him, the seeds of our design studio took root. I say seeds, as in plural, because it's important for us to express ourselves as distinct individuals—a lesson hard learned in the first year of practice.

Below and opposite: Mind Maze

Gestalt theory is key to Seán & Stephen—Stephen's ability to draw and rationalize, and his heightened sense of professionalism multiplies and enriches my pedantic compositional approaches—and together we can attract a wide variety of work: video making for the V&A Museum; a permanent installation in Walthamstow town centre, London, with Section 106 funds; a high-end specification flat renovation in London's West End. Without our divergent interests we couldn't hope to support this folio of built projects, and without teaming up we could not have won the competitions, tenders, and inquiries that led to these projects.

"Our company has two equal individuals leading it, and so acknowledging each other's strengths and celebrating each other's differences is vital."

Seán McAlister

Advice

If you have the ambition to start a practice, then I think it's a good idea to have a project from the outset to help the business grow. Seán & Stephen had a good-sized residential refurbishment project that was going to take over a year when we first started the company. This was a big benefit to give the company cash flow, something to do, and a start to building a folio.

If you do not have a project, then you need to send out lots of expressions of interest for various project types. Don't just look for architectural projects. Study the briefs, analyze what the clients are asking for, and see how you think your architectural training and skill-set could set you apart from other applicants.

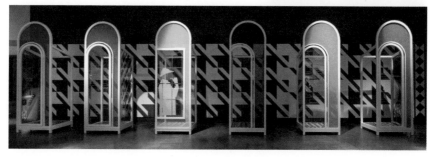

Yardhouse

Strategy:

Feel your way

Assemble

Assemble is truly unique, with more than 15 equal directors with an average age of just 22. This non-hierarchical fun-commune really is a clever approach to making dreams come true, and to prove that, contrary to popular belief, experience isn't everything—if you work hard, trust in each other, and follow your noses, true success really can come your way.

There is no predetermined recipe for such a foray into design and business; having life goals, a business plan, and company manifesto are all worthy productions, but when you are stepping outside of the typical freelance/sole-trader box, there has to be some feeling-in-the-dark first. For the first year or so, the now-named Assemble were not registered as a company, did not have a bank account, or even have a name!

For some, being involved in forward-thinking design is their dream, for others being innovative is embedded so deep in their genetics that everything they do becomes a new and exciting experience. The Assemble-rs would not have been content working for somebody else, in a traditional setting, format, and structure—for them this would have been too restricting. They need to have choice and control, luxuries that conventional employment cannot provide them with. Matthew Leung reveals their experience on the following pages.

Experience

The collective nature of Assemble is its defining characteristic. Working together in a non-hierarchical group is, in many ways, the most logical approach, and allows us to share responsibility, pool knowledge, and be productive. The mechanisms of this kind of practice are subject to constant renegotiation and have gradually evolved in the four years since our first collective endeavour, the Cineroleum on London's Clerkenwell Road.

Imagined as a marriage of two typologies in decline in city centres—the picture palace and the petrol station—this temporary project had no client, no budget, and no particular reason for being. It was dreamed up as a means of realizing a collective urge to build. In the evenings and weekends over several months, the project was slowly developed; the necessary permissions were sought, materials were gathered, plans were drawn. Armed with a minimal range of tools, holiday days, and unpaid leave (and eventually a small grant from Ideas Tap), our economy was one of many hands—working together was not only desirable, but necessary.

Below and opposite, right: Folly For a Flyover, **Opposite, left:** The Cineroleum

Nowhere was this more evident than in the construction of the Cineroleum project itself. Aside from the structure for the seating rake, which was put up by a scaffolding company, we built every element with the aid of enthusiastic friends, family, and new acquaintances made along the way. The silver curtain was made from breather membrane, obtained for free and pleated with domestic sewing machines. Wooden flip-up seats were fabricated from reclaimed scaffolding boards, and old school furniture received new in-laid formica marquetry tops. Each screening required almost every member of the group—around 20 of us—to be present, to project the film, stamp tickets, staff the bar, and, most importantly, to hoist the curtain at the end of each film to reveal the city to the audience.

At that time, with much of the group in full-time employment or education, there was little thought given to the idea that this way of working could form the basis of an alternative form of practice—there was no expectation of employment or payment, or even future projects. The Cineroleum was simply fun. The output of the collective over this period has been equally diverse, ranging from research projects to travelling exhibitions, temporary theatres to public realm improvements, housing to workshops, playgrounds to art galleries, and workspace buildings to furniture. This variety reflects the relatively large size of the collective—around 15 people now count Assemble as their primary source of employment—but also the diversity of interests within the group. There is a common preoccupation with making and the social context of design, but the general rule is that any project, regardless of type, size, or budget, is of interest if any two people feel strongly about it and are willing to take it forward.

In this way, each member works in a freelance capacity, often on a number of different projects simultaneously; it has not been practical, or even desirable, for the whole group to work on each new project in the same manner as for the Cineroleum or the Folly for a Flyover. Instead, we have retained the ideal of a flat hierarchy, but work as individuals and smaller teams who have freedom within, and can draw on the support of, the collective.

Advice

There are many talented and well-connected designers out there who will do well on their own, but for us the collective spirit was what made projects possible. Finding other like-minded individuals is key. I would also suggest that you do everything yourself at the beginning—book-keeping, meetings, clearing up, building, drawings—it is important that you have some kind of understanding of all aspects of practice as well as the life of the things you design.

Chair Arch

Strategy:

Be true to yourself

Glue Society

The Glue Society is not an advertising agency but a creative collective of writers, designers, artists, and directors who believe that concept and execution can be brought together in the same creative space, blurring the lines between art and commerce.

The whole is greater than the sum of its parts—having a team on hand to bat ideas around with, to make coffee for, to share stories, to offer up alternatives, to challenge, and to spur on is priceless. It also means that you can take on more work, spreading risk and tapping more than one field/genre. Not to mention the vibe and the camaraderie that can lift every person in any situation.

When starting a collective, it is important to set out a shared goal, a mission statement or similar, summarizing who you are, who you want to be, and the ethos behind the work you hope to produce. Once you have decided this (it could take years to refine), it is important that each member is on board, always striving for the same goal—be true to this goal with every step. On the following pages, Jonathan Kneebone describes the collective's experience.

Experience

The advertising industry has a very particular and well-trodden career path that you are encouraged to go down. You start as a junior writer or art director and work your way up via group head to executive creative director and ultimately, perhaps, to having your name on the door of your own agency. The only issue with this traditional route is that the higher up the ladder you go, the fewer opportunities you get to actually be creative. You tend to end up in meetings, steering the ship, but not actually making things. This is what motivated us to look for an alternative solution. The result was to start our own creative collective, which allowed us to both conceive and execute ideas.

Top: It Wasn't Meant to End Like This, **Above:** Knowledge Keeps Like Fish

We believe that working together can create a result far greater than any individual could deliver. One example of this is the TV show we developed and directed called *Watch With Mother*. Asked by the public broadcaster in Australia to create a new piece of entertainment, we came back to them with various ideas. However, our first attempts were perhaps more conventional than they had expected. What they were interested in was something that only we could have created, something that took our approach to commercial creativity and brought it into the broadcasting world. We worked as a group on a concept, and realized that our own brand of creativity would necessarily disorientate the audience in order to get them more deeply involved. The idea we subsequently pitched was for a sketch horror show—a world first. We took the concept of regular characters from a sketch show format, but gave each of the personalities very dark habitual behaviours. The result was a highly experimental six-part series, which managed to freak people out and make them laugh simultaneously. To make the show affordable and capable of being produced in a two-week period, each of the team at The Glue Society took responsibility for writing and directing different sketches. As a result we ended up with something that no one person would have been capable of. The show was released in app stores and has subsequently been bought and released by Sony in the US market.

Watch With Mother

Advice

The best advice I was given came from Paul Arden, who was Creative Director at Saatchi & Saatchi. He simply encouraged me to work out who I was, and then express that. Just being yourself sounds easy, but in reality you have to work at it. There are so many demands placed on you that sometimes you suppress what you really feel in order to do what you think the client or creative director wants of you. But the truer you are to yourself, the more original your work will be.

We once had reason to ask different creative people why they liked to break convention. Stephen Fry replied, "To prove that it exists". It wakes people up to the fact that things that are different are inspiring and wonderful. For us, the desire to break new ground is in our blood. We are most alive when we are doing something that has never been done before. And when you have that as a creative principle, you can't help it also influencing your attitudes to career and life in general. It is something that becomes both addictive and inspiring.

"Proving that there is such a thing as conventional behaviour is a very motivating reason to do something new."

Jonathan Kneebone

Brainstorm

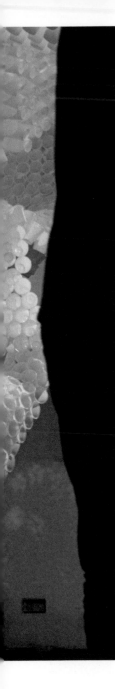

Strategy:

Push, pull, test, and tear
Red Deer

Red Deer is a perfectly mixed cocktail, where each member of the trio (Lionel Real de Azúa, Lucas Che Tizard, and Ciarán O'Brien) brings a different skill-set and interest which when shaken—not stirred—creates the perfect balance of flavours. Devised in such a way that each team player spends the majority of time doing the things that they enjoy the most and are best at, their formation has been an early recipe for collaborative working success.

Finding like-minded people is key to collaboration; you don't have to be cookie-cutter versions of one another, but having the same general outlook on the future is vital. You may not find these perfect companions at university, however, they might be colleagues, or connections made through networking.

The early stages of any collaborative start-up are exciting—all of a sudden you are living the dream, together—but it is paramount that you keep your feet on the ground as the first couple of years will require exhaustingly long hours. This exhaustion can be easier to take when you have good people around you. Even the sense of achievement can be heightened when you succeed as part of a loyal and solid team. Make memories, document them (good and bad), but always have fun. On the following pages, Lionel explains how the company got started.

Experience

Having attained our professional accreditation in architecture, we chose not to wait any longer than absolutely necessary to start up on our own. We had been taught to manage projects, contracts, and even a practice in ways that avoided taking on risk—but we did very much the opposite: we chose the name on a whim, decided to break away from our previous practice over a boozy Argentinian asado, celebrating Lucas's birthday, and pursued unusual and wondrous design projects. Soon enough we realized that the guidelines and recommendations given in Part 3 professional education did little to adequately safeguard the architect financially, nor nurture strong business acumen, but instead did much to frighten him/her into avoiding taking on any responsibility at all.

Entrepreneurship is born out of risk taking and passion. Our passion lies first and foremost in the act of designing, making, building, and producing in what we called "architecting"—unfettered by the

Lûz 2.0, Burning Man, 2014

fear of failure and at times even driven by it. Success is in the doing. We've found that doing anything with enough gusto usually leads to something profitable—and if it doesn't then at least it will have been a fun and formative ride.

Our designs usually spring from a single idea that is then pushed, pulled, tested, and torn apart—working together—each bringing a separate, unexpected view and skill-set to the table. Though it has not always been straightforward, our best designs and most memorable experiences have been when teaming up. The profession requires that the architect wears many hats—if added to that are the worries of business management and law, it becomes unmanageable, and the act of designing eventually suffers. Though we wanted to forge our own paths and learn from our mistakes, we chose to do it together through a shared passion. We thought it better to split our roles within the business to allow each of us more time to do what we love.

In the studio

Advice

I'm still too young and foolish to feel that I can impart advice on a generation. However, of late I have been appreciating the importance and fragility of time. Time is something that, if wasted, you can never win back, so I increasingly try to spend it wisely, productively, and happily.

Subverting the traditional routes has meant that the highs and lows are accentuated, but ultimately I'm free and autonomous, and that's where I'm happiest.

"Entrepreneurship is born out of risk taking and passion."

Lionel Real de Azúa

Understand the value of collaboration

Advice on teaming up from Maria Smith, Studio Weave

Studio Weave began life in 2006, emerging from a live project we delivered while studying for our RIBA Part 1. *140 Boomerangs* was an installation in a public space in the City of London as part of the London Architecture Biennale 2006 (LAB06, now London Festival of Architecture). Realizing this—our first project—was made possible through teaming up with a huge number of people, from elementary school children to experienced project managers. We learned a great deal from everyone we worked with and, most importantly, we learned the value of collaboration, which can be difficult to gain a true appreciation of while at university.

The project was one of a series of installations delivered by university students, supported by London Met's Projects Office. The Projects Office (then ASD Projects, now CASS Projects) is a chartered architectural practice led by Anne Markey. It was set up in 2004 to support students delivering live projects and offered us invaluable support in everything from professional indemnity insurance to emotional care! With this mentorship we were able to secure funding from a variety of sources, including pro-bono consultancy, in-kind material sponsorship, cash sponsorship from the City of London, and micro-funding from a long list of architecture and engineering practices. The project was made possible through an amazing amount of goodwill from a huge number of people. To be fair, I should also mention that *140 Boomerangs* was completed in summer of 2006, comfortably before the financial crisis, so securing sponsorship—both in-kind and cash—while always challenging, was not impossible.

At the time, we didn't particularly see *140 Boomerangs* as a catalyst for a practice, but more as a valuable learning experience. However, contacts we made over the course of the project led to some of our next opportunities, and the lesson in knowing when to team up stayed firmly with us. Since 2006, we have collaborated with a huge range of artists, consultants, and makers including: composers, illustrators, writers, economists, educators, various engineers, landscape architects, craftspeople, manufacturers, prop makers, sailmakers, salt producers, etc. This richness of influences has benefited our projects fantastically.

Students learning from live projects or even "on the job" have been a hot topic in recent years, especially in the light of rising tuition fees. We were fortunate enough to benefit not only from the professional support of the Projects Office, but also a substantial degree of academic freedom in the form of the Free Unit—a unit run by the head of school, Robert Mull, where students define their own projects. This allowed us to carry out not only *140 Boomerangs* as our degree project, but also to gain our Part 2 through taking on real clients alongside hypotheticals. We spent a long time working for a parental secondary school campaign group, helping them with site searches and feasibility studies for a new secondary highschool in south Camden. For us it was win-win; with minimal resources, we were able to offer clients a useful pro-bono service and we could benefit from real-life constraints and relationships.

Given this experience, I believe that education and practice could be better connected. However, the much-mooted idea of apprenticeships might be dangerous if this moves things too far away from a protected environment that's dedicated to exploring ideas. A critical weakness of education can be its isolation from the many external forces that define architecture in practice, and thereby a student's isolation from a diversity of collaborators. While prohibitively high fees might be an accelerating factor in reviewing architectural education, I believe that placing a higher emphasis on understanding the value of collaboration, knowing when to ask for help, and having a healthy respect for consultants and contractors will better equip graduates for starting out in practice.

Don't Get a Job, <u>Make a Job</u>

Gusto

To deviate from tradition takes that special something; the passion, the drive, the balls-out determination to take risks and do things differently simply because it would be harder to live with the "not knowing".

Don't make the obvious decisions—choose the least travelled path and surprise yourself in every way. Life will always throw you curve balls; these "unexpecteds" are the deviation from the norm, the happy sprinkles of oddity that transform life into lively. The trick is not just to be aware of their existence, you need to seek them out, even taunt them, and challenge them to find you.

Have big ideas and don't be afraid of them. In fact, nurture your weirdest ideas, feed them, water them, and let them grow into wild and wondrous things that no one else could ever dream of.

The following case studies illustrate some of the benefits that you can hope to experience with a combination of fearless positivity, an unbending enjoyment of your chosen field, guts, and determination.

Strategy:

Don't wait for things to happen

Mega

French art director and illustrator known only as Mega has gone to extremes to make his dreams come true. He places no limitations on himself and he truly believes that he can achieve anything. This degree of positivity, belief, determination, and willpower has served him well. He has undertaken things many others would never attempt: traversing the globe, telling little white lies to befriend important people (though of course we would never sanction breaking the law). Mega did what he had to do to get his foot in the door, and he was bold and cheeky with it. He was remembered.

He wanted to art-direct publications, so he did. He wrote his own book of his experiences and findings in New York. He didn't rely on anyone else, he didn't wait for someone to give him a job—he made his own. He created the project to showcase his skills and his knowledge, and on the back of this he was hired to art-direct other magazines. Clients and employees want to know that you can do the job and do it well, and have examples and proof to show them—Mega made sure he had these. This resolve and tenacity gave him the stepping-stone he needed to jump from working in a fast food restaurant to running his own business. In this new role as an art director Mega noticed that freelance illustrators were often unreliable, so he turned something that could have been a trial into an opportunity and produced the artwork himself, all the while keeping the clients happy and extending his own skill base and portfolio. Being able to spot niches in the market, identify opportunities, and close in on them before everyone else has had their breakfast is priceless. Be active, be busy, do things!

Lezilus Megastore

Experience

While at art school, I had no money but wanted to do things. I worked for six months in a burger restaurant in order to collect the money to buy a ticket to New York, where I went to the offices of all the people that I wanted to meet (record labels, skateboard companies, brand headquarters). I would just knock on doors and pretend to be a journalist in order to meet and interview the different actors of the so-called New York underground scene. It worked. Enthusiasm was my credibility—people would open up to me and I even ended up becoming friends with some of them. Back in France I worked a lot and produced a book called *NYC Rules*, a pretty ambitious graphic design project about the Big Apple's alternative scenes. Then I went to all of the magazine offices, with no appointment, presented what I had done, and gave them a copy of the book (everybody likes free stuff). All of the important media talked about my project and soon I was hired to become the art director of a French publication. This was the beginning of my career in the industry. People at my art school were still talking, but I was doing.

"Being able to spot niches in the market ... and close in on them before everyone else ... is priceless."

Gem Barton

Below left: illustration for
Men's Health
Right: illustration for *Complex*

What happened next

Working as an art director for magazines means being in charge of the visual aspect. I would have to find illustrators or photographers to illustrate the articles given to me by the editor. The biggest problem is that many people don't respect deadlines, and I had to wait for them before I could do my layout. I quickly realized that if you want something done, you'd better do it yourself. This is how I started replacing late visuals with my own illustrations in the magazines I worked for. I began to be noticed as an illustrator, and other magazines began ordering my artwork for their own titles.

"Don't wait for things to happen—you are the one who can create your opportunities. Draw the art you want to see, create the events you want to attend, write the books you want to read."

Mega

Strategy:

Reinvent yourself

Studiogaas

Gustavo Almeida-Santos has made unprecedented decisions in his career, and he has made every eventuality an opportunity; he has experimented with his own life. This takes guts and it will not be the ideal approach to life and work for everyone. But he didn't think twice, he didn't need to; he took every opportunity to learn something new and to reinvent himself, and when the financial crisis hit it triggered a sense of courage and survival that drowned out his fear.

For Gustavo there was a catalyst, a flashing red light in the form of a fellowship award that could not be ignored. If you are lucky, you too will get such a clear sign. This, however, is not always the case. For some, the catalyst is much less obvious, more subtle, and unassuming. The key is to always be aware, be expectant; if your eyes are not open and you are not susceptible, the opportunities will pass you by.

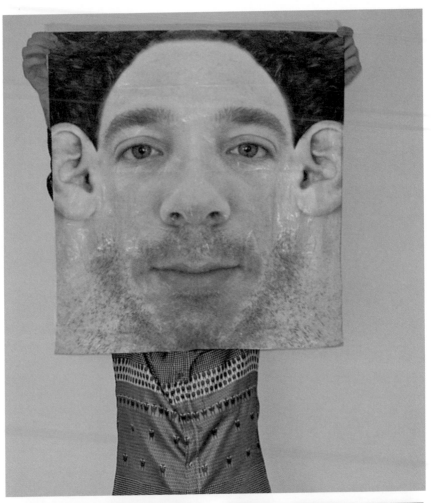

Skin trash bag

Experience

It was not by accident that I decided to leave my country, where I had my own studio, my friends, and a more stable financial life. I simply could not keep going with "not knowing" what could happen if I gave up everything and tried new things over and over again.

Everything started when I was awarded a fellowship in 1999, and had to choose between three cities: Barcelona, Milan, and Belgrade. I chose Belgrade because it seemed *not* to be the obvious choice. I went there and worked for a small architecture studio. Great experience, until we all (international students, fellow friends) were kicked out of the country due to UN intervention. After that, I went back to Brazil, sold all my possessions, and flew to Los Angeles to stay with a friend for a break. This ended up being the best ten years of my life. That's when I finally broke through and did all of the things that I wanted to do: I went to art school, worked for an American office, did my first projects in the US, showed my work in galleries, met people, learned how to use a whole array of software, experimented with technology, etc. But again, after ten years I felt the urge to keep going, to reinvent myself, to put myself in unknown situations. That was when the opportunity to do a project in Algeria came up, and I didn't even think about it twice. Of course it was not simple,

Tanq, kiosk design

as I had to first convince the non-profit agency that my project was the best one, which I did. And of course it was not easy to learn French in the four months before the trip!

After that I moved to Spain, got married, and had to reinvent myself again in a new country that was in economic crisis. I think that when you have to start your life over and over again, as I did, and on top of that you have to face a financial crisis, all of this triggers a sense of courage and survival, and the fear disappears. In Spain I was able to work with artists, design exhibitions, design stores, finish my master's, and I finally started my PhD in researching fashion shows.

Advice

If you have to show your portfolio to someone, highlight your ideas instead of your technical abilities. Don't be scared of trying and don't listen to your parents when they tell you that you need a stable job in a stable company. Get out of your comfort zone, even if that means accepting a weird but exciting job in Madagascar!

Schools are great, you learn tons of things … but they have their agendas and they are corporations. Be careful. If you want to subvert the traditional routes, you have to know your career really well in order to play the game—and that means you have to have experience, you have to fail; you have to try things over and over. You have to know yourself really well in order to understand what is best for your well-being or desired state of mind. That is why I constantly put myself outside of my comfort zone. In order to subvert, you need to have a professional and personal structure. Otherwise it is impossible.

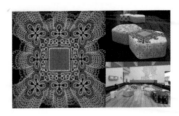

Textile design with Queensland Art Gallery

"You have to know yourself really well in order to understand what is best for your well-being"

Gustavo Almeida-Santos

Strategy:

Create positive change

Arbuckle Industries

Ian Harris, co-founder of Arbuckle Industries along with David Krantz, left architectural practice after three years because he believed there to be a great void in how the public views and engages with architecture. This realization left him feeling unfulfilled by professional practice, and he turned his attention to creating positive change.

Ian found a passion for using film as a medium to make this change through storytelling, creating something that led toward this goal of engagement and awareness. Along with ex-colleague David, Ian began making a film about architecture school—hoping to help close the gap between public perception and the realities of becoming an architect.

The pair saw a genuine niche in the market, so they put everything on the line; they gave up jobs, borrowed money from family, and took on any work they could find to build up a folio of projects to showcase. In the early days you might have to take on work that may not live up to your dreams, but remember that momentum is a very powerful force. On the following pages Ian explains how starting slowly and building up pace naturally enabled them to grow sustainably.

Behind the scenes on a shoot

Archiculture poster

Experience

My evolution from architecture student coming out of design school in Ohio to the co-owner, producer, and business director of a video production company based in New York City has been a long process of gut-wrenching lows and euphoric highs. It all began sitting across from another guy who was fresh out of college, with an idea to make a documentary film about architecture school. To our surprise no one else had yet done such a film and we thought "why not us?".

After learning the standard technical skills of filmmaking we raised all the money we could from small firms, friends, and family members and then quit our jobs, leaving behind careers we had been trained and paid for. Along the way the economy collapsed, we were lied to by key partners, stolen from by collaborators, and we felt completely isolated, having left everything and everyone to make our idea a reality.

When we started we did anything we could—websites, graphics, photography, but mainly focusing on video production. We didn't always know exactly what we were doing, but we knew that we needed to be doing something we believed in and apply our creative talents to make something, anything. Today we have grown the company into a stable business and are positioned as the leading architectural video production company in New York, with work around the globe.

It is not in my nature to ask someone else to provide me with my professional and creative happiness. Every company is veiled behind their name, logo, and brand, and to find a truly fulfilling environment and culture takes time that I was too impatient to spend. At the end of the day, you need to feel fulfilled and the timeline of the building industry was too slow for me, along with the detachment from feeling and engaging the user, so I jumped ship to create my own path. If what you want to do is already being done by someone or by a company then go work for them, but if you cannot find that then you must create it yourself.

Advice

The older I get, and the more experience I gain as a professional, the more I believe in a process of highly structured and focused team work and brainstorming, followed by directly responsible task-oriented management of resources. Architects can be seen as the orchestrators who bring together extremely skilled teams to solve complex, unplanned problems while ensuring the structure and direction is there to bring the solution to fruition. The past, where master builders guide the entire design and building process, is no longer the way we work, nor what society needs.

Arbuckle film: *Robert de Niro*

When the economy tanked in 2008, this is when most young and unemployed architects were able to start making an impact and creating clients out of non-traditional business models. Architects need to get out from the office and engage the community to solve problems locally and build a capacity in their community for better quality of life and built environment.

My situation required me to create my own business to support the kind of work and impact I wanted. I feel great reward from growing a business but it is always fraught with risk and uncertainty. Some people can sustain themselves and mature in this type of scenario, but it doesn't suit everyone. Ask yourself what works for you and your lifestyle, while being aware that these can and will change as you grow and age. As long as you're honest with yourself and believe in what you're doing then you can find your career path. Mentorship, connections, and professional associations will go a long way in enabling and supporting you, so be sure to keep these progressing in parallel.

"If what you want to do is already being done by someone or by a company then go work for them, but if you cannot find that then you must create it yourself."

Ian Harris

Strategy:

Keep on learning
Something & Son

Only take on work that you know you can do, right? Wrong. Andrew Merritt and Paul Smyth of Something & Son see every new commission and every new conversation as an opportunity to learn a new skill.

For many students, an art/design foundation course is the most beneficial learning environment—one where you are enabled to discover how you work the best. Something & Son see their working life as a foundation course for the professional world; its art, its design, its architecture, its "Something".

This may seem a little drastic to some, learning on someone else's time and dime—but why limit yourself to things that you already know? What better way to push yourself, to expand your knowledge base, and experience as many areas of the design industry as possible? You may well discover that you are brilliant at everything, or at the very least, something. Andrew explains why every day is a school day!

Rooftop Fish & Chips shop,
Folkestone Triennial

Experience

I couldn't and wouldn't be employed by anyone, as I was idea driven, and no one is going to employ an ideas person—that means being the director/head honcho/founder, and who's going to employ a graduate to be one of those? I had to go it alone and start my own projects.

I believe that throughout a project I should be learning something new, and with Something & Son projects we often throw ourselves in at the deep end. By doing this we are naturally taking the harder route, but the end return is much more satisfying and our general knowledge and skill-set have grown.

When we took on FARM:shop, (an inner-city growing space in Dalston, London, which was built to reinforce the link between country farms and urban populations), we didn't know anything about farming or anything about the future technology involved such as aquaponics. We were all holding down other jobs and we had a tiny budget, but we had free rent and a clear idea of what we wanted to do. The idea hit a zeitgeist and, without any pushing from our side, we had international press coming down, which we used to encourage people to give us stuff and deliver it quickly so they didn't miss out on the press. Through in-kind support and donations we raised the initial £5k budget to an £80k project. The project was contracted to exist for three months; four and a half years later it's still there, now paying rent back to the council.

When we began working on the Barking Bathhouse we had never designed a building before, and we aren't architects, but our idea needed a piece of architecture. Aided by a large budget, within seven months we had turned an initial idea into a fully functioning self-purpose building providing spa treatments to the public. The project involved us designing a building and its interior, devising treatments and an experimental

"Take every opportunity you get by the horns and push the project to its absolute max … make that £1k project look like it had a £10k budget, as that will get you the next project with a £15k budget. And so on…"

Andrew Merritt

Barking Bathhouse

spa experience, managing the construction process, becoming spa licence holders, hiring everyone from bar staff to manicurists, devising a series of events around well-being, and creating a website with a ticketing system. With the budget we made sure we didn't need to recoup money from ticket sales so were able to charge locals £2 and people outside of the borough £8 to use the spa facilities.

For our Makerversity project, together with two others, we were given an opportunity to take 20,000 square feet of space in Somerset House but with no funding. A learning and making space for pioneers and prototypes—we had to decide if we were willing to take the risk with our time and try to make the project work or not. For the first four months we worked for free, but soon money started flowing in; members started using the space early on in the project, so while we were still pulling at the carpet, people were using Makerversity. It made for an intense experience as it gave us the freedom to do the project and allowed for the project to organically grow. We now have 150 members and have the whole space functioning. The next step is to carry on improving facilities.

Top: Sweat Oratory
Above: Gravel Bay

Advice

Think long-term—you're going to do more projects, so your portfolio is only going to get bigger; you're only going to learn more while others give up, meaning by the end you'll be the last one standing. Make sacrifices to meet your end goal. A career is mostly step by step, with the odd lucky big jump.

Remember that everyone, from a director to a contemporary, is in the same boat; everyone wants to succeed and needs help … what can you do to help them and help yourself at the same time?

You can't count on money to encourage you to get up in the morning

Advice on gusto from FREAKS freearchitects
(Guillaume Aubry, Cyril Gauthier and Yves Pasquet)

After some years of working abroad in different architecture practices, one day the three of us decided to launch our own practice. This did not correspond to winning a commission for a building, but to winning an award from the French Ministry of Culture (AJAP Prize). We want to underline that we did not start by working on a building project—as is usually the case—but rather by starting to look for projects. This is exactly when you have to add some gusto to the recipe; without enthusiasm and self-motivation, you can't count on either money or good feedback to encourage you to get up in the morning. Launching a business from scratch takes both courage and faith.

It might sound romantic to consider gusto as being the one and only ingredient required to run a practice and be successful, but there are lots of architects in the world. The good thing is that we are mostly quite good at what we do, the bad is that we are all so inspired by the ever-increasing amount of look-alike architecture images we see on the Internet that we produce a more and more homogenous style of architecture. We FREAKS don't believe in revolutionizing architecture, we just want to achieve our projects by being sincere, smart, and efficient. Once the project is built, the second part of our story starts: documenting and promoting the project. That is when we really pull out all of the stops. We could just take a nice set of pictures and send them to some blogs and magazines. No risk. So why do we go the extra mile? To prove to the rest of the world that we are in the game? To prove to ourselves that we are in the game? The answer is much more selfish; it is much more fun to write a new scenario for each photoshoot, even more so when we perform ourselves to activate the space/building. Distorting and questioning what a good architecture picture should be gives us so much pleasure that we consider it part of our job.

Whatever the scale is, whatever the fee is, what counts is being able to pick the projects that you really want to work on. We are very lucky to work in a field in which our job blends seamlessly with our pleasure and leisure. But don't forget to protect your own private life. What is the point of designing a restaurant, a bar, a cinema, if you do not have a minute of free time in your weekly routine to go out and experience it for real?

Getting the most out of your education

"School is not an analogue for what some refer to as the 'real world'—the world of work, of doing things and being paid for them, for projects whose lives exist beyond institutional studio walls, crit spaces, and end of year shows. School is a world unto itself, a different kind of place where different kinds of things happen. The idea that school prepares you for the world is both right and wrong. Does it make you employable? Turn you into someone who can slot into a team and effortlessly begin delivering projects? Certainly not, that's a whole other issue, one that only time and painful experience will give you."

Sam Jacob, Founder of FAT Architects, now Principal at Sam Jacob studio

What is education (for)?

When we look past accreditation and grades, education is really about accepting and understanding transformation. It is not about pitching up in your first year of study as a fixed entity, but rather as an individual who is alive and hungry for knowledge. As educators, we endeavour to create a safe environment for our students to learn in. Remaining still and steady in a sprinting world can be seen as reliable, but also potentially risky. The design industry requires a spread of approaches to innovation in teaching—from the traditional to the radical, and everything in between—in order to provide a spectrum of learning opportunities for a variety of creative individuals. It is important, as a student, to realize that just as all students are not the same, neither are all professors or indeed universities.

For a good student, education is about questioning your relevance, your goals, and your position in the world. Teaching (in any environment) is so pivotal to the development of society that it must be given a regular spring clean. A good educator is dedicated; they care about their courses and their students, they consistently update their lectures and case studies, and renew project briefs to stay relevant, to challenge and improve themselves, and to be instigators of social and cultural change rather than followers of it.

How to make the most of your education

At school, your learning was primarily the responsibility of your teachers. As an adult attending university, that responsibility is yours. Education is an active endeavour, not a passive exercise. Being present and listening is a good start, but is not enough. In order to fully gain from education, a student must engage with every aspect of a learning lifestyle, as laid out in this chapter. To get the most out of your higher education you must see your time at university as a place for intellectual adventure rather than an obstacle course of credential-shaped hoops that you are forced to jump through.

In countries where students must pay for university, education has been incorrectly compared to a commodity. Information is disseminated from your tutors in lectures and seminars, but more general conversations happen daily—formally and informally—in the studio, in the lift, in the cafeteria queue, and you must embrace this incidental learning. Never again will you be amid such diverse and gifted educators. The more you are exposed to your tutors, the more you can learn from them. Sitting in class and not engaging in a two-way interaction doesn't work, it is not enough to just be present.

You have to learn to listen. Not simply hear. Real listening, and by that I mean critical listening, is very different from passive listening such as listening to the television or the radio. Critical listening requires additional engagement; it requires you to think about what you are hearing while you are hearing it. A good way to develop critical listening skills in lectures, seminars and tutorials lies in the way you take notes. Copying down the information delivered verbatim is simple passive listening, a shortcut to forgetting. In order to learn something, the information must pass through at least one state of change; in doing that the information enters the brain with significance. For example, when I was a student I tried (and still do) to transform content delivered to me verbally into diagrams. Doing this means that you are critically looking for patterns in the information; you are being forced to recognize relationships, similarities, and differences. Now you are thinking, listening, learning, questioning, and evaluating all at once!

You need to take in information in order to generate knowledge, but the two are not mutually exclusive—listening in lectures and reading the assigned books will provide you with information but will not give you knowledge. Information is, in simple terms, data with meaning. Knowledge requires cognitive engagement, process, and analysis—the ability to mentally collect and collate information in a way that makes it useful to you and to others, identifying and speculating on the presence of patterns within the information. In order to become knowledgeable you need to put in the legwork, you need to practise the techniques, read around the subject, and take time to think about and digest the information, as well as seek out additional information of your own.

The more information you have, the more knowledge you can generate. We can always know more, so our learning should never stop. You and any future employers also have a responsibility to continue your learning. Should you become an employer one day, remember this: to develop a strong, powerful, and tactical workforce you need to continue to grow as individuals and as a team. Training provides information, but that alone will not nurture development. Skills have to be taught and then practised, allowing for multiple applications across different design fields.

In design education, the "critique" experience is often the one that students have most concerns about and fears of. The best way to describe a critique is as a formal and invaluable tutorial, although I have heard many students describe it as something much more crude and traumatic! In critique situations it is important that you are prepared, stay calm, and do not get defensive (you're not a superstar just yet). The best thing that you can do is to listen: you do not have to take the advice, in fact showing that you can distinguish between the useful and the less useful demonstrates that you are in control of the destination of your project work as well as your personal development.

Sometimes, in order to progress, we need to understand the value of downtime. Isaac Newton famously developed numerous theories during his time studying at Cambridge University. What is less well documented is that many of these breakthroughs came during the late 1660s, when the University was closed due to the outbreak of the plague. It was during this time—when Newton had no access to the library or the facilities—that he had time to truly stop and think, time to piece together all the things he had been taught and find their relevance. In this time he developed his theories on calculus, optics, and the law of gravity. Studying at university is intense, and the vacation periods are intentionally long so that they give you time to rest, recuperate, gain alternative experiences, and prepare for the new semester. Use your vacation time wisely, get the balance right; if you work too hard you will burn out, but if you don't do any work you will lose momentum and be slow off the mark.

Universities are communities of people, more than of facilities, but, just as you are exposed to thousands of different people during your degree studies, you can also access dozens of facilities. Be sure to make the most of all that is on offer; ask nicely, broker deals, call in favours, trade skills with others—you are unlikely to be able to access (at no extra cost) such a wide range of equipment and amenities in one place ever again. Get as much experience as you can and expose yourself to everything; this way you will have the widest foundation possible, enabling you to make the most informed decisions about your future. Exposing yourself to such a variety of educators and facilities will allow you to experience real collaboration and discover whether a life of creative diversity might be for you.

Preparation for the (real) world

Nowhere in a design-course handbook will you find a university claiming to train specifically for the "job". Universities teach people how to think, not what to think; they're a learning experience, not technical training. Learning doesn't stop once the course is completed; graduates have the responsibility to continue their own life learning through experimentation. The world becomes your classroom.

The education system is not a production line, and the industry cannot order graduates complete with selected ingredients: this kind of approach would stifle and smother industry advancement. Both professionals and the media have pedaled this idea to the extent that almost everyone believes it. Founder of Ford Motors Henry Ford famously said, "If I had asked the customers what they wanted they would have said, faster horses". Providing people with what they think they want/need isn't always the smartest move for society and innovation. This is one of the fundamental problems we encounter when the receiving industry does not always fully understand the university system. Universities were developed as places for invention, research, and development and to foster, nurture and harbour innovation. The following quotes underline this philosophy:

"[Architectural] education is always under scrutiny from the profession, about creating 'office fodder' as it were. Good students will learn quickly and in a good studio they will promptly become very useful. I look for imagination, flexibility, and good communication skills, in a broad sense. If they don't know something I expect them to be able to know where to find it."
Will Alsop, OBE RA, winner of the RIBA Sterling Prize

"We are not educating students to fit in with the 'reality' of out-of-date professional practices. Skills also develop over time, with practise, in practice. If a practice considers itself to be 'modern' it should also take seriously its responsibility to keep supporting its employees' skill development."
Ruth Morrow, Professor, Queen's University Belfast

"One of the problems facing schools is that they try to simultaneously reflect and direct the needs of practice: producing oven-ready graduates conditioned to meet the needs of business 'as is,' who are also equipped with the skills needed to move practice forward through innovation and entrepreneurship."
Dr Harriet Harriss (RIBA) Principal Lecturer,
Oxford Brookes University

"Education should not aim to prove the profession, but rather there should be significant points of contact and radical points of difference between professional training and disciplinary positioning."
Perry Kulper, Associate Professor, University of Michigan

Teaching Entrepreneurship?

After reading this book you might be thinking that universities should provide students with relevant "entrepreneurial training", allowing graduates to enter the world as the case studies in this book have. Actually, I always say that there are courses in business and entrepreneurship available, should people want to study them, but generally I'm a believer in maximizing on current situations, and design degrees (yes, all of them) to a greater or lesser extent provide their graduates (and drop-outs) with many of the skills needed to do this. Take the case studies in this book, for example: they had no extra training, and it is because of this that their drive and passion is so admirable. You can seek out and cultivate entrepreneurial experiences in your own education without going on a dedicated entrepreneurship course. If everybody was trained to think "innovatively", innovation as we know it would die. In order for progression to continue to take place, the masses must be led by the few. The few will continue to forge their own path, taking what they have learnt and reappropriating it into a super-hybrid of itself, a manifestation never seen before.

You should embrace the things that non-entrepreneurs will shy away from; prioritize experience over product, face risks daily to build up your tolerance, pursue the moments of messiness and instances of volatility. In doing this you will become conditioned to look for the unusual, to see the world in ways that others cannot, to challenge the obvious and irritate the oyster. There is much you can learn from a design education—skill, technique, passion, foresight—but the most important thing that you can take with you for the future is the vision and belief that you can change the world.

Credits

The author and publisher would like to thank the following institutions and individuals who provided images for use in this book. In all cases, every effort has been made to credit the copyright holders, but should there be any omissions or errors the publisher would be pleased to insert the appropriate acknowledgment in subsequent editions of this book.

Author's acknowledgments

I wish to personally thank Graeme Brooker and
David Dernie for supporting me, believing in me, and
recommending me to Laurence King Publishing, where
Liz Faber and Gaynor Sermon have made my dream of
becoming an author a reality. I would like to thank my
wife Carly and our family for their support though the
tough times and for giving me the strength to reach into
the emotion of my past, which provided me with much
of the desire and dedication to write this book.

I must also thank all of the friendly advisors who have
provided encouragement and suggestions during the
research period—you know who you are—and, of course,
the myriad of incredible contributors who have dedicated
their time and faith to the project.

Thank you.